The French connection
– 100 years with Danish architects at l'École française d'Athènes

Acts of a Symposium held in Athens and Copenhagen 2008 by l'École française d'Athènes and the Danish Institute at Athens

The French connection
– 100 years with Danish architects at l'École française d'Athènes

Acts of a Symposium held in Athens and Copenhagen 2008 by l'École française d'Athènes and the Danish Institute at Athens

Edited by

Erik Hallager & Dominique Mulliez

Monographs of the Danish Institute at Athens
Volume 13

The French connection
- 100 years with Danish architects at l'École française d'Athènes
Monographs of the Danish Institute at Athens
Volume 13

General Editor: Erik Hallager
Graphic design: Erik Hallager
Printed at Narayana Press

Printed in Denmark on permanent paper
conforming to ANSI Z 39.48-1992

The publication was sponsored by:
l'École française d'Athènes
Ny Carlsbergfondet

ISBN: 978-87-7934-567-6
ISBN: 978-2-86958-219-4

Distributed by:
Aarhus University Press
Langelandsgade 177
DK-8200 Århus N
www.unipress.dk

De Boccard Édition-Diffusion
11, rue de Médicis
F-75006 Paris

Gazelle Book Services Ltd.
White Cross Mills, Hightown
Lancaster LA1 4XS, England
www.gazellebooks.com

The David Brown Book Company (DBBC)
P.O. Box 511
Oakville, CT. 06779, USA
www.davidbrownbookco.uk

Illustration on front over: Reconstruction from the 4th century
Temple of Apollo, Delphi, by Erik Hansen (see his article Fig. 9)

Contents

7 Preface

9 Introduction
Dominique Mulliez

11 The relationship between the Beaux-Arts School and the French School at Athens
Didier Laroche

19 The topography of a monument. Delineated observations in Delphi
Gregers Algreen-Ussing

33 Une pierre à Delphes
Erik Hansen

41 Étude et publication d'un matériel spécifique : le cas des terres cuites architecturales de Delphes
Christian Le Roy

55 Ce que j'ai appris au contact des architectes danois
Jean-François Bommelaer

69 The theatre at Delphi and the Reykjavík City Theatre
Þorsteinn Gunnarsson

81 The Dansih architects and their contribution to ancient and modern architecture
Martin Schmid

95 Conversations with a French architect – present meets past, creating future
Torben Thyregod Jensen

108 Map

Preface

The year 2008 was the centenary for Danish architects working for the French School at Athens. The first architect was Gerhardt Poulsen, who came to Delos in 1908 and since then 73 Danish architects and students of architecture from the Royal Danish Academy of Fine Arts, School of Architecture, have worked for the French School at 14 different locations in Greece and one in Cyprus. The event was jointly celebrated by the Danish Institute at Athens and l'École française d'Athènes with a large exhibition and an international seminar both in Athens and in Copenhagen where the exhibition was displayed at Thorvaldsen's Museum and where the seminar took place in the room with French sculptures at the Ny Carlsberg Glyptotek.

The eight contributions in this volume is the outcome of the seminar. It presents a mosaic of aspects concerning the Danish architects. Why did it all start, how did the architects work, what did their work mean to the French archaeologists and architects, and how did their work with ancient architecture influence on their future life?

The authors were free to choose French or English language for the publication – two languages with different typographical rules. The editors agreed on a compromise in that the French contributions by and large follow the French rules, while the English contributions by and large follow the Anglo-Saxon rules and occasionally also the guidelines of the series.

The editors are grateful to the authors of the volume for their good collaboration. We wish to thank Ms. Anastasia Caramanis for correcting the texts in the English contributions. We want to repeat our gratitude to the Foundations that made the project possible: Carlsbergfondet, Realdania, Ny Carlsbergfondet, Augustinus Fonden and Dronning Margrethe og Prins Henriks Fond. Last but not least we are grateful to the sponsors of the publication: our respective schools and the Ny Carlsbergfondet.

Athens, November 2010
Erik Hallager & Dominique Mulliez

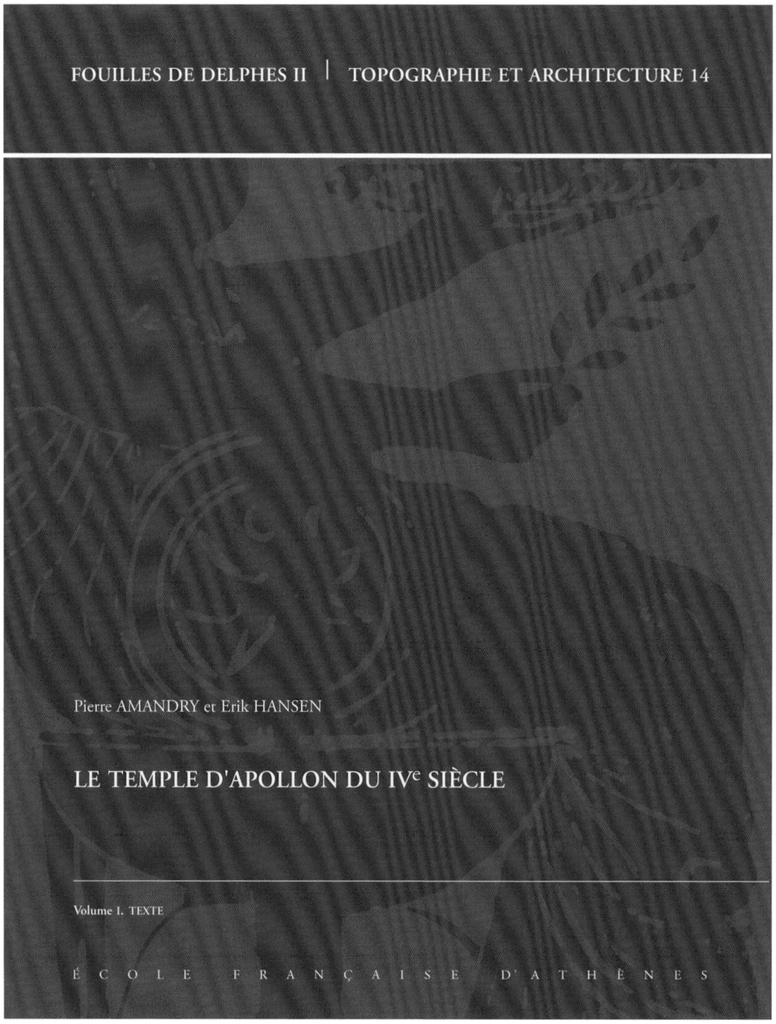

La publication, dans la série des *Fouilles de Delphes* II. – *Topographie et architecture*, de l'étude du temple d'Apollon sous la double signature de Pierre Amandry et Erik Hansen apparaît comme l'aboutissement ultime de la collaboration entre des architectes danois et l'École française d'Athènes.

Introduction

Dominique Mulliez

En 1908, après avoir vu les relevés du jeune architecte danois Povl Baumann, qui travaillait à Lindos, Maurice Holleaux, alors directeur de l'École française d'Athènes, prit l'initiative d'écrire à l'Académie des Arts de Copenhague et proposa d'accueillir chaque année un architecte danois : l'accord qui s'ensuivit marqua le début d'une longue collaboration, qui profita principalement aux sites de Délos et de Delphes, dans une moindre mesure à ceux de Malia en Crète et d'Amathonte à Chypre. Le 18 octobre 2008 à Athènes, le 6 décembre 2008 à Copenhague, une journée d'étude accompagna l'inauguration d'une exposition destinée à célébrer le centenaire de cette collaboration[1]. Des chercheurs, des amis, architectes ou archéologues, qui avaient partagé en Grèce ou à Chypre des projets couvrant parfois plusieurs décennies et qui, pour certains d'entre eux, ne s'étaient pas revus depuis de nombreuses années, se sont retrouvés ; de plus jeunes ont découvert à cette occasion des visages derrière un nom connu.

Ces acteurs ont décrit les prodromes et les étapes d'une histoire désormais séculaire. Ils ont également exploré les divers aspects d'une méthode qui, pour reprendre l'expression d'Erik Hansen, est « le résultat d'une évolution que nous pouvons suivre à travers les cent années (...) et qui reflète aussi, dans ses grands traits, l'évolution de l'architecture durant ce dernier siècle ». Enfin, ils se sont interrogés sur les apports mutuels de leur collaboration. Car tel est bien l'enseignement que l'on tire des huit articles issus de ces rencontres : si les archéologues et les architectes de l'École française d'Athènes, Didier Laroche, Christian Le Roy, Jean-François Bommelaer et Martin Schmid disent ce que fut l'histoire de cette relation et son apport pour les dossiers dont ils avaient la responsabilité, si Erik Hansen et Gregers Algreen-Ussing restent, chacun à sa manière, fidèles à l'architecture antique, Thorsteinn Gunnarsson et Torben Thyregod Jensen rapportent ce que l'expérience athénienne leur a apporté en retour, dans leur vie professionnelle et personnelle. Malgré – ou à cause de – la diversité des approches, il importait de restituer ces interventions : fondées sur une expérience partagée et parfois singulière, elles apportent une contribution significative à l'histoire de nos disciplines et àla réflexion que doivent poursuivre architectes et archéologues sur leur indispensable collaboration.

Martin Schmid conclut son article en rappelant qu'entre 1856 et 1873, l'École française d'Athènes occupa une vaste demeure située Place Syntagma, à l'emplacement du futur hôtel Grande-Bretagne, – la Maison lemnienne, dont l'architecte était danois et s'appelait Théophil Hansen : avec l'avantage que procure le recul du temps, il y voit comme un signe, « an auspicious omen », de la collaboration à venir. Le 27 septembre 2010, était organisée la présentation du volume des *Fouilles de Delphes* consacré au *Temple d'Apollon du IVe siècle*, sous la double signature de Pierre Amandry et Erik Hansen : avec la publication de cet ouvrage, un cycle se termine indubitablement. Il revient aux jeunes générations d'en inventer un nouveau, avec des moyens et des méthodes renouvelés, mais sans oublier jamais la dimension humaine de nos entreprises, « tant il n'est de richesse que d'hommes ».

1 Voir E. Hallager & D. Mulliez (éd.), en collaboration avec G. Algreen-Ussing, M. Schmid, E. Chairi et S. Riisager, *Den franske forbindelse – 100 år med danske arkitekter ved Den Franske Arkaeologiske Skole i Athen / Une liaison française – 100 années de présence d'architectes danois à l'École française d'Athènes / Δεσμοί με τη Γαλλία – 100 χρόνια παρουσιάς Δανών αρχιτεκτόνων στη Γαλλική Σχολή Αθηνών* (2008).

The relationship between the Beaux-Arts School and the French School at Athens

Didier Laroche

The relationship between the architects of the *Beaux-Arts* tradition and the French School at Athens is commonly considered a failure, due to their divergent attitudes to ancient architecture. At first sight there seems to be a conflict between the old fashion that was characterised by the architects of the *Beaux-Arts* on the one hand, and, on the other hand, the scientific new approach of French and foreign scholars at the beginning of the 20th century. Of course there is some truth to this: it is possible to view the collaboration that the French archaeologists began with the Danish architects in 1908 as a conscious break with the artistic approach and more highly criticised tendencies of the *Beaux-Arts* architects.

However, if we look more closely at the events of this period, we can also find other reasons for these changes – reasons which have nothing to do with problems of cooperation or misunderstanding between the archaeologists and *Beaux-Arts* architects. Firstly, we should remember that the dramatic events of the 20th century – especially the two World Wars – also affected the architectural profession. Many young architects were killed in the First World War, including, for instance, the highly talented Adrien Martinaud, who worked in Delphi during the early 1910s. On another note, Henri Ducoux was an architect who came to Athens because the crisis of 1929 had created a high rate of unemployment in France. He left Greece in 1943, after ten years of successful cooperation and activity with the *École française d'Athènes*, because he knew there was a need for architects in the reconstruction of France's devastated areas. He became a very busy, official *architecte de la reconstruction*. Both cases demonstrate the difficulties that the *École française d'Athènes* faced in finding young French architects.

Apart from the political upheavals of the time, the period when the French School began its collaboration with Danish architects was also a turning point in the history of architecture. Tony Garnier, who was then *pensionnaire* at the *Villa Medici*, created a scandal in 1903, when instead of submitting the requisite *restauration* of an ancient monument or city, he proposed a design for a "contemporary city". Some historians consider this event to be the symbolic starting point of modern architecture. As a matter of fact, a deep rift between architects and archaeology began to develop in France after this clash. Nevertheless, it would not be accurate to say that the Danish architects hired by the *École Française* took the place of French architects; the contribution of architects like Albert Gabriel, Adrien Martinaud and Henri Lacoste, all of them fully trained academically in the *Beaux-Arts* tradition, was also appreciated by the archaeologists during this period (Fig. 1).

It is useful to go back to the 19th century and consider the role of Greek architecture in the edu-

Fig. 1. Henri Lacoste, in F. Courby, *FD* II, *Le temple d'Apollon*, pl. XIV, "Linteau de la porte." In reality, this freeze belongs to a baldaquin situated in the cella.

cation of French architects. After the Greek War of Independence, the Greek Revival movement flourished in most European countries, especially England, Germany, Austria and, of course, Greece. This movement was less important in France. The French Academy in Rome insisted on the pre-eminence of Roman architecture and French architects had developed their own eclectic style, now known as *style "Beaux-Arts"*. The fact that the French architects did not refer to their work as the Greek Style, as did their English and German colleagues, can help us understand why they showed less interest in the study of classical Greek architecture.

Before we examine this issue, we should briefly outline the work of the French architects in Greece, both outside and within the French School at Athens, throughout the 19th century. A detailed study of the architects working for the French School has already been made by Marie-Christine Hellmann[1] in her article published for the 150-year anniversary of the *École française d'Athènes*. Philippe Fraisse has also completed academic research on the work of the architects in Delos,[2] which provides very useful information not only about their presence, but also about their methods and the way they elaborated reconstruction drawings.

Many years before the *École française d'Athènes* was created in 1846, French archaeologists and architects had participated together in early travels to Greece in order to document the architectural remains of classical antiquity. Pre-empting Stuart and Revett's publication of *The Antiquities of Athens* (1762) by four years, Julien David Le Roy was perhaps the first of the French architects who purported to give a precise account of the most celebrated buildings of Greece with his *Ruines des plus beaux monuments de la Grèce*. As had been the case one century earlier with the antiquities of Rome, every scholar or artist claimed that his own drawings were more accurate than those of his colleagues.

Among the earliest travellers to return with drawings and descriptions of Greek ruins, we should of course cite Choiseul-Gouffier. Generally however, the work and drawings of the French were influenced by Romanticism, whereas more accurate drawings were made by English artists sponsored by the *Society of the Dilettanti*, or the Germans, like Haller von Hallerstein whose work still remains partially unpublished.

After the French Revolution, the *Académie Royale d'Architecture* became the *École Nationale des Beaux-arts*. As a result of this, the teaching of architecture was clearly linked with the other arts and became completely separated from the academic system of the universities.[3] The most successful architects won the *Grand Prix de Rome*, which gave them the opportunity to study in Rome for four years. During their stay in the *Villa Medici*, they were required to complete a study of a classical building every year, with the *envoi* in the fourth year being the most important. However, the same period also saw the creation of the *École Polytechnique* and the *École des Ponts et Chaussées*. In these two institutions, architecture was taught using a more technical approach, in contrast to the artistic approach of the *Beaux-Arts*.

Viollet-le-Duc had been appointed as a teacher in the School of the *Beaux-Arts*, but his rationalist understanding of the history of architecture provoked riots and he was obliged to quit the school. His ideas were later propounded in the *École Polytechnique* and the *École des Ponts et Chaussée* by the outstanding historian Auguste Choisy, who wrote his monumental *Histoire de l'architecture* in the last decades of the 19th century.

At the turn of the 20th century, another rift began to take place, this time between architects and engineers. Drawings submitted by the *Beaux-Arts* students at various competitions (the *Grand Prix de Rome* was just one of these, but of course the most prestigious), show nothing about the structure of the buildings, which remains a void. In contrast, the paragons of the rationalist movement, Viollet-le-Duc and Choisy explained the evolution of architecture mainly by way of technology.

At the beginning of the 19th century, some students of the *Académie de France* in Rome travelled to the south of Italy and Sicily (Henri Labrouste,

[1] Hellmann, M.-Chr. 1996, 191-222.

[2] Unpublished.

[3] This is the reason why the French architects still depend on the Ministry of Culture and not on the Ministry of Education like in other countries.

Fig. 2. Abel Blouet, *Expédition de Morée*. Restitution du temple d'Égine, 1838.

Paestum, 1826) to see Greek architecture, which had gained favour with the work of Winckelmann, although they were not officially allowed to travel to Greece until 1845.

Even though the Roman model was the real paradigm for the *Académie des Beaux-Arts*, the lack of interest from the Academicians is a little surprising because during the same period, there were other architects, who had not won the *Prix de Rome*, but had gained respect by studying the architecture of antiquity (such as, for example, Charles Texier who travelled in Anatolia and Persia in 1834).

We should also mention here Jean-Nicolas Huyot, a pioneer in this field, who was the first to teach the history of architecture in the *École des Beaux-Arts* after he had returned from his travels in Asia Minor and Egypt (1817-1821); most French architects of the 19th century studied under Huyot. Chief member of the *Expédition de Morée* (1828-33), was the architect Abel Blouet who published an important work on the subject in 1831 (Fig. 2). Blouet had been the first to undertake excavations in Olympia (1829). It has been said that the creation of the *École française d'Athènes* was an indirect result of the *Expédition de Morée*.

The *Grand Tour* became a tradition for artists and architects. At the same time, Auguste Chenavard, who was to become the appointed architect of the city of Lyons, travelled to Greece and Anatolia with his colleague Dalgabbio and the painter Étienne Rey. His drawings and his work are the focus of some forthcoming academic publications.

The first work undertaken for the *Prix de Rome* in Greece concerned the Acropolis (1845, Théodore Ballu and Alexis Paccard), prior to the foundation of the *École française d'Athènes*. The work was performed without the collaboration of archaeologists and the results were better appreciated for the technique of the drawings than for the study of the buildings themselves. Nevertheless, in 1851, the archaeologist Raoul Rochette gave a positive account of the architects' work in Greece. It is notable that most of these studies, and especially the written descriptions of the work, have now fallen into neglect. Apart from the work undertaken for the *envoi de 4e année*, other studies were also made, as some of the architects had become friendly with the archaeologists they met during their travels in Greece, and continued to collaborate with them after their stay in Rome. Among these architects were Albert Thomas (publication of *La vallée du Latmos* with Oliver Rayet, 1877), Louis Bernier (Halicarnassos) and Emmanuel Pontremoli (*Pergame* with Collignon, 1900; *Didymes* with Haussoulier, 1904), who built the famous neoclassical *Villa Kerylos* on the French Riviera.

Fig. 3. Albert Gabriel, *EAD* 16, *Le Samothrakeion*, fig. 106, "The Sanctuary during the first period."

During the first years of the *École française d'Athènes*, a Beaux-Arts section was open mainly to architects awarded a *Grand Prix de Rome* and offered them participation in surveys and excavations. However this section was closed in 1874, beginning a period of uncertainty concerning the participation of architects in the programs of the *École française d'Athènes*.

Nevertheless, Henri-Paul Nénot was appointed to the first excavations in Delos which started in 1873, thanks to the funds given – it is worth remembering – by the *Société Centrale des Architectes*. Later, in 1927, Nénot became a symbol of academic architecture, when he won the competition for the new building of the *Societé des Nations* in Geneva. At that time, the modernists who believed that Le Corbusier should have won this competition decided to create the *Congrès International d'Architecture Moderne* (CIAM). While working on this project, Nénot was assisted by a younger winner of the *Prix de Rome*, Camille Lefèvre, who had also previously worked in Delos, in 1909; Danish architects started to work in Delos at the same time.

The exhibition of the recently discovered drawings of Albert Gabriel[4] (Fig. 3) demonstrated the influence of the Danish architects on the work of this prominent historian of architecture, who eventually founded the *Institut français d'archéologie* in Istanbul (1930). The Danish architects introduced the three-dimensional views (perspective or isometric) which were not highly regarded by the Beaux-Arts tradition, following the recommendations of Alberti.

André Hilt in 1937 and Jean Debuisson in 1946 and 1948 were the last winners of the *Prix de Rome* to work with the French School. Although neither of them stayed for a long time or even fully collaborated with archaeologists on any publications, their presence shows that there was still a link between the French Academy in Rome and the French School in Athens.

Albert Tournaire (*Grand Prix de Rome*, 1888) was the official and only architect to assist the excavation team during the so-called "great excavations" in Delphi (1892-1902). Tournaire published the first volume of the *Fouilles de Delphes* under his own name, but does not appear to have collaborated with any of the scholars, except the Director of the French School, Théophile Homolle. Until recently, Tournaire's restoration drawings (Fig. 4) were subject to fierce criticism from archaeologists involved in Delphic research.[5] He won awards during the International Fair held in Paris in 1900, but his presence in Greece was

[4] *Albert Gabriel (1883-1972), architecte, archéologue, artiste, voyageur*, Yapı ve Kredi Yayınları, Istanbul, 2007.

[5] In the archives of the EFA, we can find polemical letters addressed to the director G. Daux and directed against the archaeologist Pierre de la Coste-Messelière.

Fig. 4. Albert Tournaire, Study for the interior of the temple of Apollo in Delphi, *c.* 1900. Archives EFA.

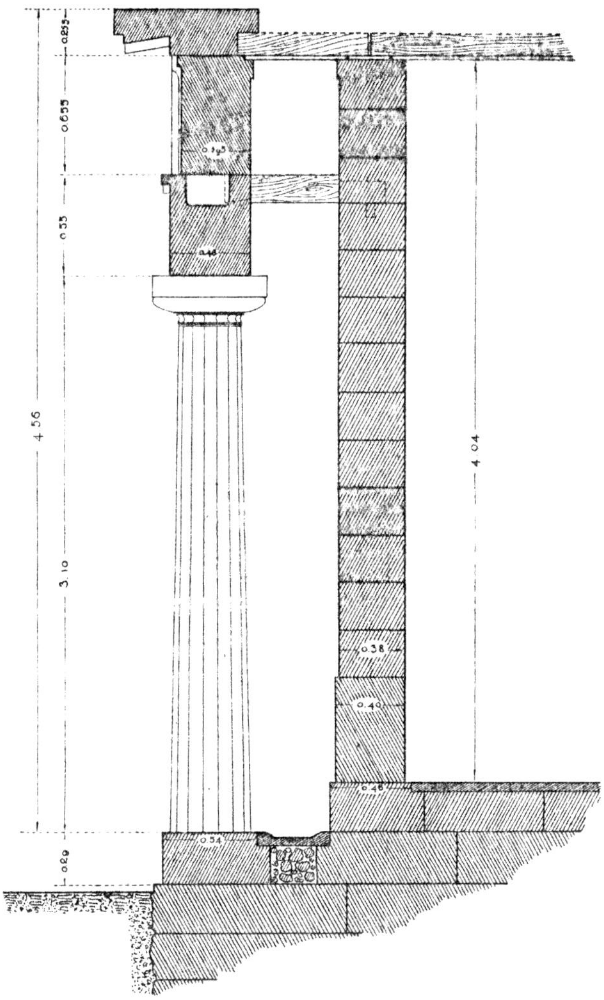

Fig. 5. Jean Replat, Restored section of the archaic tholos in Delphi, *c.* 1922, Archives EFA.

not compatible with his official duty after returning to France.

In the first decade of the 20th century, we see the names of some French architects who were of less importance, although some of them did remarkable work. Adrien Martinaud, already mentioned above, went to Delphi as a young architect in 1910 and 1911 and successfully studied a great many monuments there, especially the tall pillars and the Etolian twin columns. As Martinaud was killed during the First World War, few of his studies were ever published. M.-Chr. Hellmann also mentions other architects, among whom were two women, Yvonne Dupuy and Madeleine Charléty.

Jean Replat, though he was trained as a topographer and not an architect, has a special place in the first decades of the 20th century, not only because of his most famous work – the reconstruction of the Athenian Treasury in Delphi (1905) – but also due to the tremendous number of studies and restorations he undertook, first at Delphi (Fig. 5) and afterwards in Delos. His drawings were not pleasing from an artistic point of view, but he probably had the greatest talent for joining the dismantled parts of a building back together. After a suicide attempt in the 1920s, he lost his sight and died in 1933.

We have already mentioned Henri Ducoux, who was appointed official architect of the French School in the 1930s. He would dash from one site to the other, directing the restoration of ancient buildings (the Tholos and the temple of Apollo in Delphi) or building houses for the French School. Like Albert Gabriel earlier in Delos, his drawings are clearly influenced by the new style introduced to the *École française* by the young Danish architects. At the same time, because it was hard to find young French architects interested in archaeology or because they asked for excessive salaries, the French School hired Russian architects expelled by the Revolution, like Youri Fomine (Fig. 6) and Konstantin Tousloukof. Even though they came from the same country, these architects working

Fig. 6. Youri Fomine, architectural details, from Daux, G., *FD* II, *Les deux trésors* (1923), planche 27.

for the French School do not seem to have been closely involved.

In conclusion, I would propose that the presence of the Danish architects at the *École française d'Athènes* is more due to the fact that French architects had begun to lose interest in Greek architecture at a time when, on the contrary, the Scandinavian modern classicism exemplified by so many Danish architects, provided an opportunity to approach the artistic spirit of ancient Greece in a new way. The catalogue of the exhibition held by the Danish Institute shows some examples of a correlation between the drawings of these young Danish architects and their own building designs. It would be very difficult to find such examples in the *Art Deco* or Modernist movements which prevailed in France in the 1920s, or even in the classical reaction which followed in the 1930s, but displayed a monumentality that was once more influenced by Roman models.

Bibliography

Blouet, A., A. Ravoisié, A. Poirot, F. Trézel & Fr. de Gournay, 1831-1838
Expédition scientifique de Morée, ordonnée par le gouvernement français. Architecture, sculptures, inscriptions et vues du Péloponèse, des Cyclades et de l'Attique, mesurées, dessinées, recueillies et publiées (3 volumes), Paris.

Hellmann, M.-Chr., 1996
'Les architectes de l'École française d'Athènes', *BCH* 120, 191-222.

Le Roy, J.D., 1758
Ruines des plus beaux monuments de la Grèce, Paris.
Digital copy at: http://diglit.ub.uni-heidelberg.de/diglit/leroy1758/ 0001?sid=a3466c132589b3de5b0b55ba6733f08b

The topography of a monument. Delineated observations in Delphi*

Gregers Algreen-Ussing

Abstract

The article describes the survey that was carried out in the years 1963-67 at the sanctuary of Apollo in Delphi. With a brief reference to earlier survey entries of the area, the groundwork for such an extensive task will be discussed against the topographical criteria, scale, fixed points and signatures chosen for a specific survey. Thereafter, this process, which in the Danish survey tradition has been called the "analytic" method, will be explained with reference to examples and the tools that are used in the task. The article is concluded by a recollection of the thoughts that were tied to the purpose and the use of the survey forty years ago.

The French connection

One of the earliest attempts in Denmark, to draw a reliable map of the country was undertaken in the 18th century. It was published in Erik Pontoppidan's *Danske Atlas* of 1763, which aimed "to give a detailed historical and chorographical description of all Danish provinces and towns in general".[1] According to one Frenchman, it was also well overdue.

The Frenchman in question was Lacombe de Vrigny, who in 1702 had travelled the country, where he – obviously – encountered the need for good maps. However, in reference to Danish cartography, he wrote in his account of his journey: "It were to be wish'd every body made Maps of their own country only, but the *Danes* are too lazy for that, and rest statisfy'd with what the *Dutch* tell them".[2]

King Frederik V was surely aware of this critique, because not only did he support Pontoppidan's work, he was also enthusiastic about the topographical mapping of the whole country, which in those very years was under discussion in the then newly founded *Royal Danish Academy of Science and Letters*. The mapping was to be carried out according to a French model – the French were the first to apply the triangulation method to create a map of an entire country. Vrigny's wish was apparently not in vain, as this took place in the 1740s, and it is in this connection that we learn about the use of the theodolite, which thereafter became a crucial instrument in all topographical surveys.[3]

One hundred and fifty years later, French cartography once more showed off its distinguished tradition in Delphi, where Apollo's sanctuary was uncovered beneath the many culture layers that had been deposited over thousands of years at this site, once considered the hub of the universe and now being visited again by all sorts of people. I refer here to the outstanding work that the Frenchmen Henri Convert and Albert Tournaire carried out for the French School at Athens (Figs. 1-2).

Cartographic preparations

Likewise, for the survey that is the topic[4] of this account, it can be said that French cartography served as a model as far as the trigonometric method is concerned, where the theodolite, logarithmic tables and geometric formulas were the fundamental tools.[5]

---

* I am grateful to Sine Riisager for translating my Danish text into English

1 Lembech 1961.

2 Vrigny 1707.

3 Kejlbo 1972.

4 Hansen, E., G. Algreen-Ussing, 1975 (Atlas).

5 Today, theodolite, logarithms and formulas are substituted by electronic equipment.

Fig. 1. Self-portrait (?) from 1902 showing Tournaire marking fixed points at the Apollo temple in Delphi with his theodolite, notebook, and surveyor's staff, detail. (From Tournaire 1895, pl. VIII = *Atlas* F).

Fig. 2. Topographical map of the village Castri from 1892, where the Apollo's sanctuary hides beneath numerous culture layers from generations of settlement. Convert 1897, pl. XIX = *Atlas* A.

The survey was initiated by the architect Erik Hansen in 1962 by means of a small stencilled notice posted at The Royal Danish Academy of Fine Arts, School of Architecture in Copenhagen, announcing that students of architecture interested in undertaking a survey for the French School at Athens should report to him. The survey of the sanctuary of Apollo in Delphi was to last about 3 months and take place in the summer of 1963. With reference to this laconic note on the students' bulletin board, it is notable, in hindsight, that the survey lasted 4 years. Even more surprising is the confidence shown by the initiator that such an extensive and difficult project could be executed by students in the midst of their studies. But this confidence was characteristic of Erik Hansen's indomitable optimism, which rubbed off on all the participants of the survey and the work that followed in the years from 1963 to 1975, when the finished atlas was printed.

One of the first decisions one must make with regard to a survey entry is the scale, which in the case of the sanctuary of Apollo at Delphi was determined at 1:50. This meant that the finished map of the sanctuary would be almost 4 metres high and 3 metres wide. Of even greater significance is that the choice of scale determines which phenomena can be drawn onto the map and is therefore a consequence of the analytic perspective that one wishes to convey in the reading of the map. Furthermore, not all phenomena at a given location are relevant, even if they can be drawn in the chosen scale. The selection of scale becomes further complicated, since it has to be made prior to the commencement of the survey and on this premise can potentially exclude conditions that would contribute new information about the site. Here I would like to note that these considerations do not become any easier now that we have new electronic equipment, but on the contrary, require furthermore that the built-in programs in the electronic devices used – which in themselves contain a selective recording of the surrounding world – must be made subject to a critical evaluation.

All these considerations and choices are summed up in the list of signs, which, so to speak, constitutes the grammar that forms a readable syntax in the map. My point in these general considerations about the method of cartography is that this grammar must be created all over again every time a map has to be drawn – something which also happened in this case.

Moreover, this sanctuary was, and still is, a very special place, about which much has been thought and written since antiquity. In this connection, the Danish king's attitude to mapping in the 18th century is thought-provoking. He commended Erik Pontoppidan's chorographic description with the following statement:

> "Here, many words could not describe as much as a glance at the map, and at a drawing of cities, buildings, antiquities, provisions or such things as a description just by words in this matter would be too copious and even unclear." [6]

We could take this insightful commendation made 250 years ago and inspired by France's trigonometric survey as an auspice of the fruitful collaboration that since 1908 has developed between French archaeologists with their historiography and the Danish architects with their surveys;[7] a collaboration that secured new and optimum conditions for the future with the foundation of the Danish Institute at Athens in 1992.

The geometric order

As indicated, a cartographic survey consists of an exchange of information between the observer and what is actually observed at the given location, based on a previously defined context. Added to that is an abstract element which consists of the geometric order in which this exchange takes place. The trigonometric starting point for this order in the survey of the sanctuary was made as a straight line of 130 metres, spanning across Apollo's temple, with terminal points in the sanctuary's ring walls to the east and west (Fig. 4, line 220). From this baseline, 60 fixed points were set for the 20 sub-planes, which were then marked in the terrain by

[6] See above, n. 1.

[7] Hallager & Mulliez (eds.) 2008.

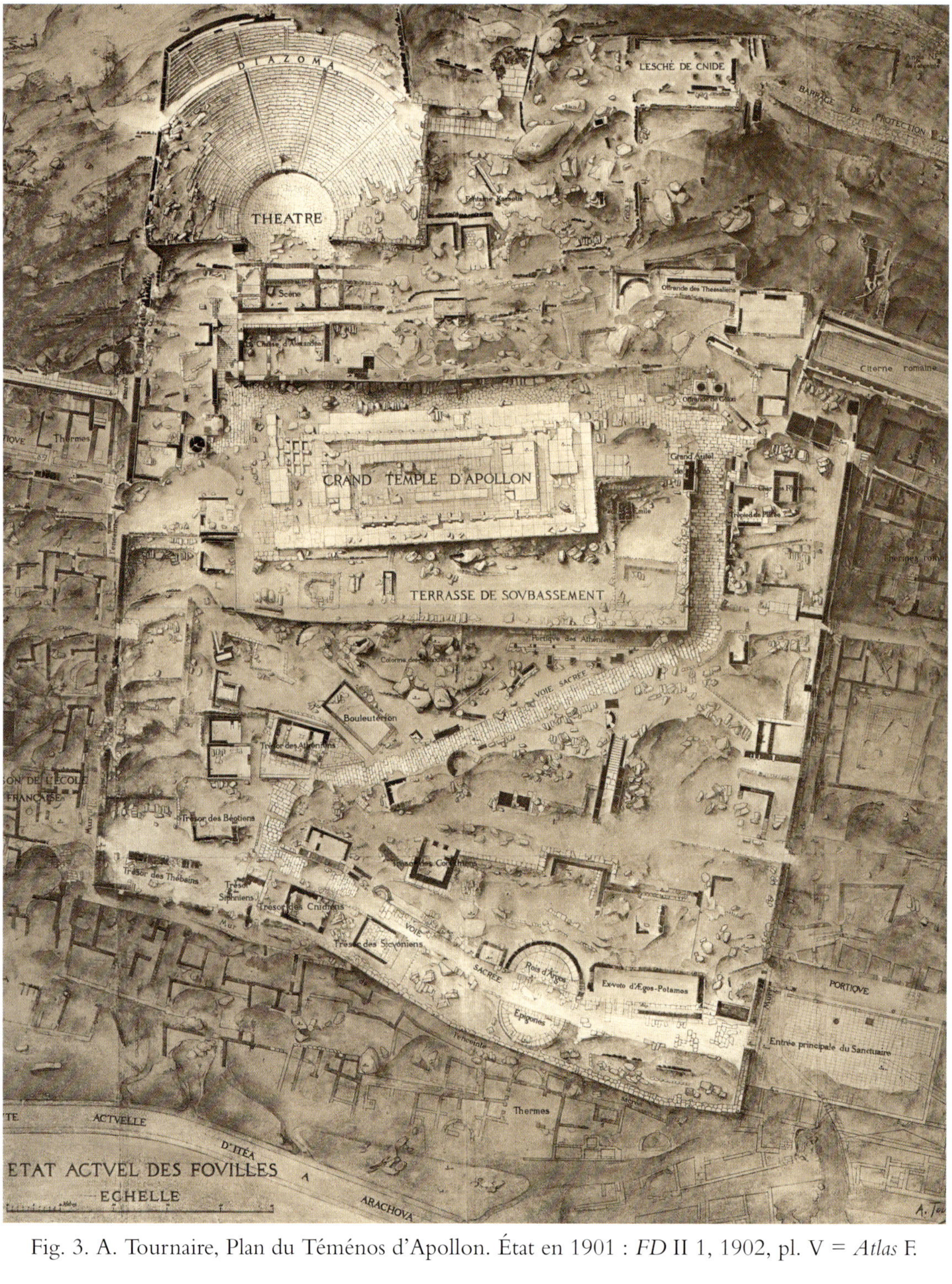

Fig. 3. A. Tournaire, Plan du Téménos d'Apollon. État en 1901 : *FD* II 1, 1902, pl. V = *Atlas* F.

cast-in or embedded brass sprigs in the sanctuary.

These then were the basis for 30 fixed points that were used in the 17 sectional views. These, a total of 90 millimetre exact reference points, were all determined in a spatial system of co-ordinates, the arbitrary datum point of which lies outside and beneath the area of the sanctuary, which means somewhere in the air above the valley, where it –

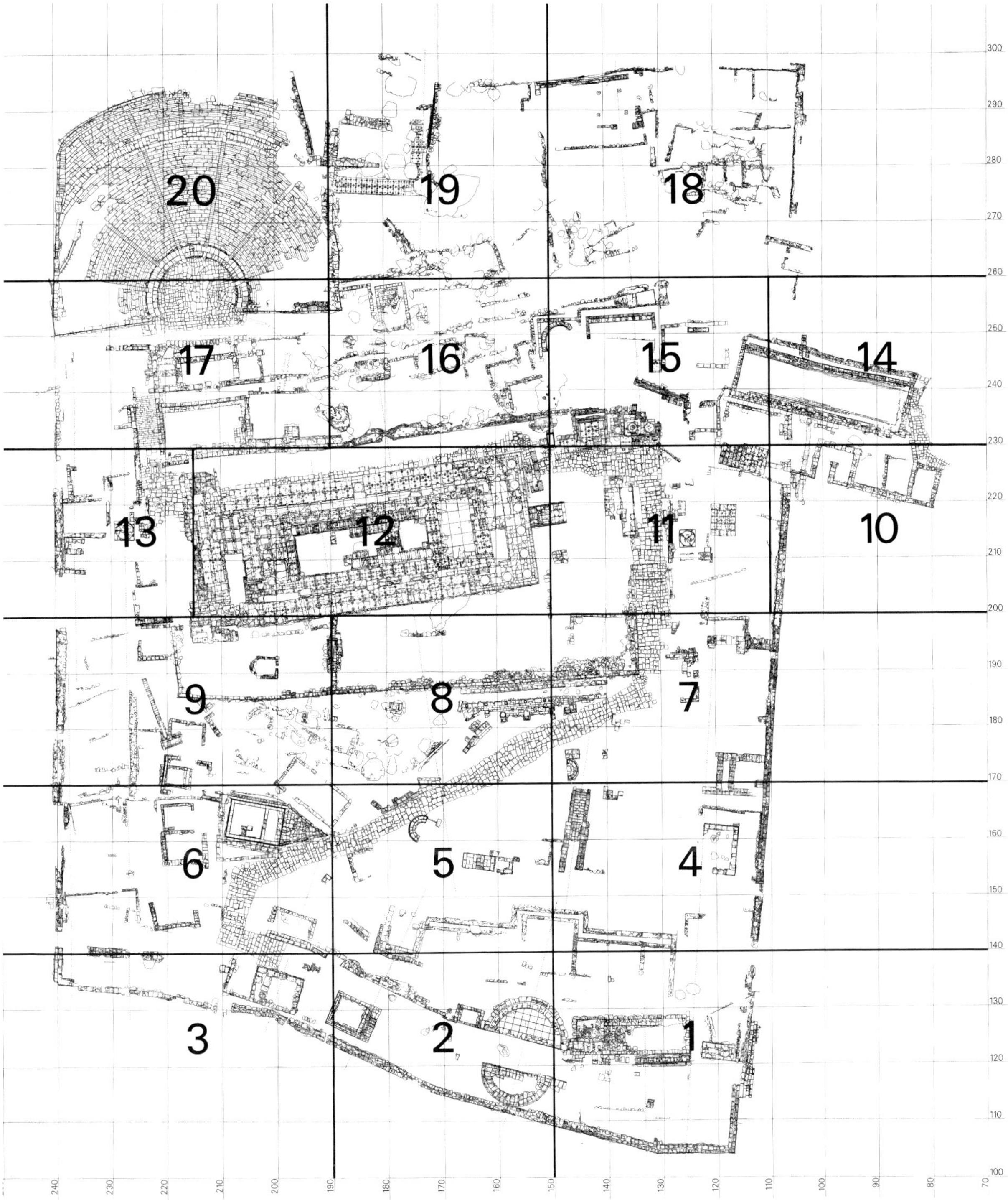

Fig. 4. The relation between the geometric order and the delineated observation. When comparing Tournaire's map of the sanctuary from 1902 with the one produced in 1967, the accuracy – the one determined by the geometric order – is the same. However, the drawn information framed by this accuracy is completely different. Hansen, E., G. Algreen-Ussing, *Atlas* III.

together with the baseline – makes up the starting point of a quadratic ten-metre net, upon which the sub-plane division is based.

In other words, this abstract reference-net can be found again and can, in a re-survey, not only show whether this unique monument on the hillside

Fig. 5. Delphi 1963. Erik Hansen, with the "tea cosy" hat, surrounded by students from the first year, standing on monument 511, The Thessalian base. A total of 22 students, divided on two campaigns in 1963 and 1964, participated.

is in motion, but also, whether the paper in the publication due to humidity or the like may modify the scale of the drawing. The marked fixed points in the terrain can thereby become the base for surveys in the future. Before the individual stone circles could be surveyed and drawn at a scale of 1:50, some common principles as to what to survey and what not to survey in the individual sub-planes and sectional views had to be agreed upon among the participants.

The result of these agreements was, first of all, that each sub-area in the survey referred to the closest fixed points, so that inaccuracies were not transferred to other sections. Furthermore, according to topographic tradition, measures were not to be entered on the drawn phenomena.

Secondly, surveying and drawing on the paper were to take place on location and only on location. The survey and its interpretation of the phenomena had to be finished, so to speak, *in situ*.

Thirdly, only artificial phenomena were to be included in the survey; that is stones *in situ*, as far as they were part of a specific stone circle and construction, or were placed with the intention of restoration. In the sectional views, the closest stone circles behind the sections were to be included based on the same criteria.

Fourthly, the survey entry was only to include stone circles from before the Roman period, based on the references made by the archaeologists.

These four main rules may sound like obvious instructions to the 22 people who participated in the survey.[8] However, the individual guidelines hide the very crucial difference between the interpretation of a monument by a sole individual and an interpretation comprised of several parts, each interpreted by a different person, and which, in the end, will have to be put together as a unified whole to form an atlas.

It was therefore very provident that the French School at Athens took the second rule literally. In the years 1964 to 1967, the director Georges Daux generously placed the school's building

[8] Hallager & Mulliez (eds.) 2008, 89.

within the site at the disposal of the survey team for the subsequent drawing in pen of the planes and sections that had been measured. Thus, quite unusually, this significant process was closely connected with the fieldwork survey and made it possible to resolve matters of dispute in the compound drawing of the 20 sub-planes and 21 sectional views, through further examination of the excavation field itself.[9] The director's support for this work became evident when, among other things, he had hot water installed in the bathroom and kitchen, saying: "You don't live in Delphi in the winter. Only Vikings would do that".

An exception had to be made as to the third rule, for the sanctuary of Ge. It contained several naturally formed rocks that would have been difficult to exclude from the survey, as they were probably a part of the nature sanctuary that determined the significance of the site. The large rock boulders resulting from landslides, in the northern part of the sanctuary, also had to be incorporated, in order to give a clear impression of how the superposed constructions were sited.

Distinguishing between nature- and culture-phenomena thus proved to be not so simple and probably not entirely appropriate in the topographic survey of a monument where information about the landscape could reveal the natural conditions that determined the monument's tectonic structure, materiality and form, and the work process that had created it. I will return to this point below.

The delineated observation

Although the geometric order is based on instrumental devices which develop day by day in increasingly fast and more extensive electronic programmes that replace the manual operations, the delineated observation is totally different. The delineated observation is conditioned by a "slow empathy" which opens up to a phenomenological interpretation and demands craftsman-like skills on the part of the observer to reproduce it.

The surveys in 1963-67 followed the guidelines that Erik Hansen had used in his long standing work on the Siphnian Treasury and which he called

Fig. 6. Drawing tools used in 1964-1967 for drawing in pen of the surveys from 1963 and 1964.

the "analytical" approach.[10] Hansen's strongest influence was Einar Dyggve's "sterile" way of drawing, which this architect and archaeologist had developed in the inter-war years.[11]

The plan drawing consisted of a rectangular vertical projection on a horizontal plane, and the sectional drawing of a horizontal projection rectangular on the section plane. The sectional drawings were produced by raising the plan drawings from the projection as elevations through the measuring of the site. Using this procedure, it is necessary to accept severe foreshortening in both plan and section views, which in Delphi included more than 200 stone circles, which were comprised of the retaining walls, fundaments and constructions selected by the archaeologists on the basis that they were believed to date from pre-Roman times. When its positioning was fixed in the topography by means of the geometric order, each stone became the object of a detailed survey.

In this connection I would like to cite another Danish architect, Steen Eiler Rasmussen, who was a significant mentor for both Erik Hansen and the students who participated in the survey. In a small pamphlet about the observation of the architecture, he wrote:

"To see a thing, one must display a certain

[9] This work was carried out in 1964-1967 by A. Bramsnæs and G. Algreen-Ussing.
[10] Hansen, E., 2000.
[11] Dyggve, E., 1955.

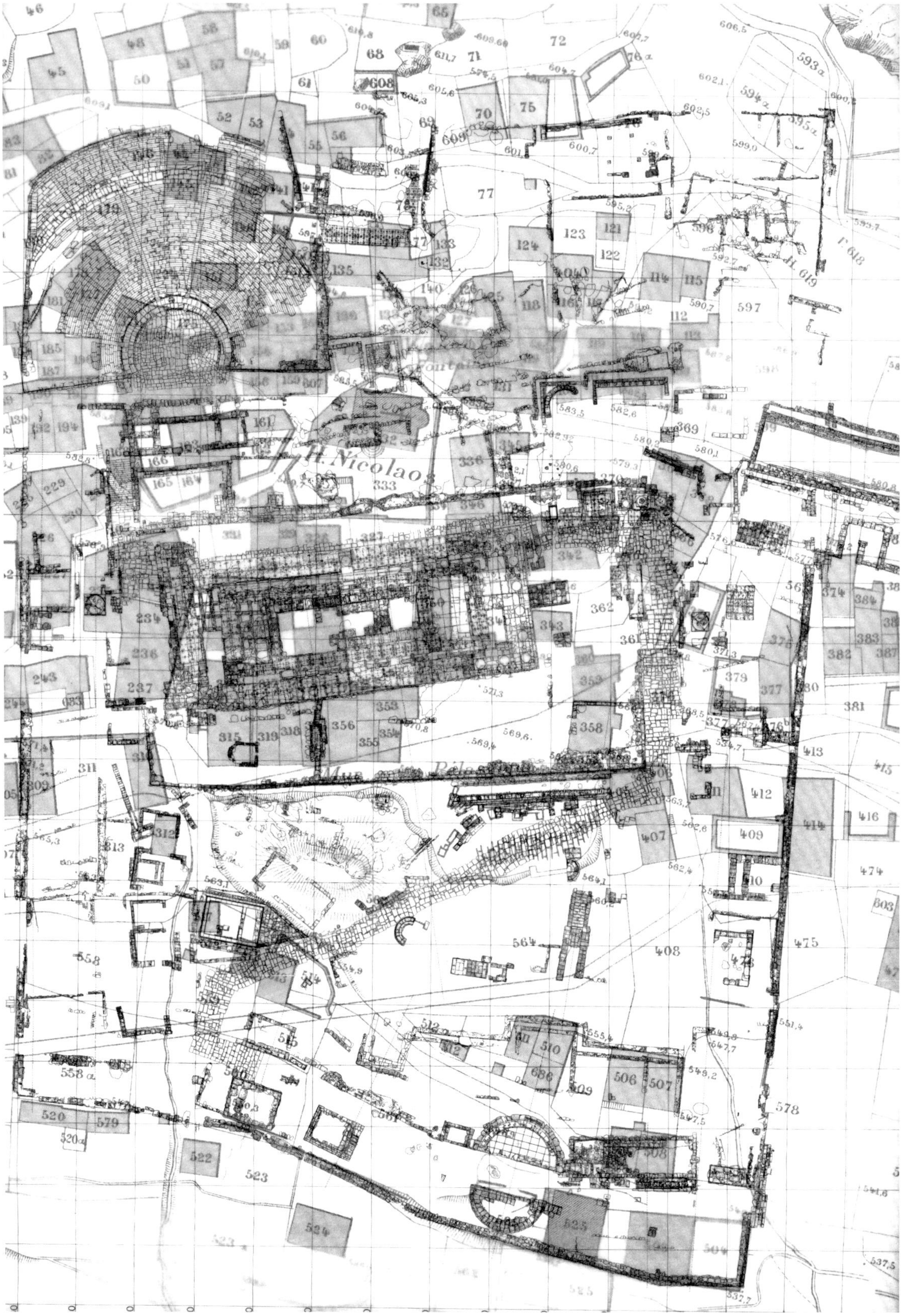

Fig. 7. The sanctuary's antique carbon in the village Castri's structure. Compounding of Convert's plan 1897 and Hansen's plan 1975, with the Athenians portico as a starting point. *Atlas* H and C.

Fig. 8. The successive destruction of the village Castri surveyed by A. Tournaire 1894-1902. *FD* II 1 (1902), pl. VII.

activity. It is not enough that a picture is created in the mind's eye. In order for it to come alive, one must work at depicting what one sees — reproduce it. When one contemplates a building, one builds it in one's mind, and the more active one is, the more one observes."[12]

In terms of the survey of the sanctuary, the reproduction that Eiler Rasmussen describes is of a quite special nature. It revolved around the tools that once left traces showing the procedure in the existing building process from antiquity. As mentioned earlier, Erik Hansen calls his method of survey "analytic" and this can be understood in several ways.

Firstly, this method can be understood as the penetrating observation of the physical contour of the building stone and the phenomena that can be measured on it. Here, the contour is drawn first, then the pushing – or lifting – holes, the hewed out recesses for cramps, module markings and the adaptation of load-bearing surfaces, which can all be classed with the tectonic function of the stone in the building structure. Secondly, how the stone was hewn is indicated by the signatures left by the different tools that performed it: the blunt hammer used in the rough stone, the sharp axe in the soft porous stone, the point chisel and the tooth chisel and, finally, the small flat chisel for the fine finishing. The tools leave detailed traces of the building process: the lifting, pushing and pulling of the stone in order to then attach it to the other building elements using cramps and mandrels. In contrast, the random fractured surfaces of the stone are left blank.

It is thus evident that this procedure not only provides information about the tectonic function of the stone in question, but also about the work process it was subjected to.

Thirdly, the information obtained about the building process and its organisation can potentially tell us something about the social conditions that applied at the time of construction and which can be as interesting as the appearance of the building in question, once it was completed.

The topography of a monument

The collocation of the words "monument" and "topography" in the title of this short account serve to signify that a survey of this kind may have been able to contribute to the topographical surveys made in the course of time, reaching beyond the individual building. Naturally, the overall character of the atlas work led to premature discussions that not only included the nearest surroundings and their history, but also

[12] Rasmussen, S. E., 1934.

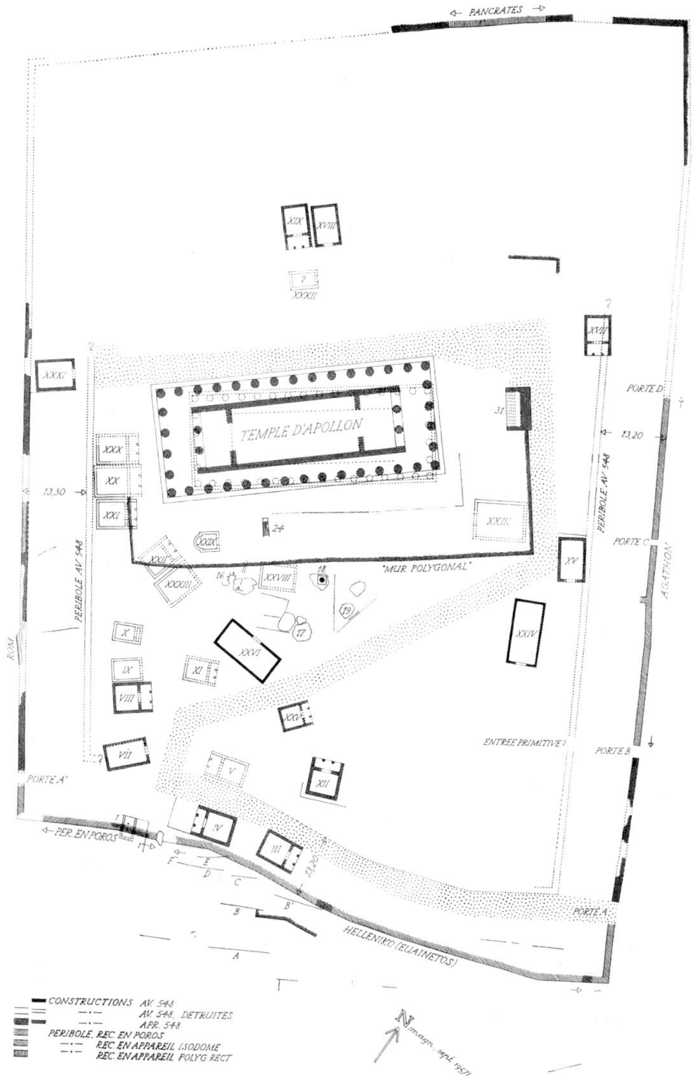

Fig. 9. Hansen, E., Le sanctuaire d'Apollon vers 500 av. J.-C. *BCH* 86 (1960), Appendice, "Les péribols du sanctuaire d'Apollon à Delphes", fig. 68.

the significance of the regional landscape for the sanctuary and its construction, which motivated many excursions. Several years later, I have become aware that both before and since the atlas work, research within these areas has been made in a way that we, as students of architecture, did not have the means to match.[13] I will just mention three fields of study which, parallel with the actual survey of the sanctuary shown in the atlas at a scale of 1:100, led to a series of supplementary key plans and an air photograph that prefaces the publication.

The first topic that was discussed during the survey concerns a story that took place in contemporary times. With reservations as to the cartographers' observations and ways of drawing, 11 maps at a scale of 1:500 covering the period from 1887 to the actual atlas survey, show the changes that took place in the constructions of the sanctuary as they were uncovered. One can observe both the appearance of reconstructed additions and the disappearance of other constructions.

A particular aspect of this story is Convert's plan of the village Castri, which takes us back to the time before the excavations began and Tournaire's successive survey, stage by stage, of the destruction of the village. With this unusual foresight to document the condition of the site before their own intervention altered it, we now have the opportunity, in a subtly backward way, to contemplate the structural interaction between

[13] E.g. Bommelaer, J.-Fr., 1992. Rousset, D., 2002.

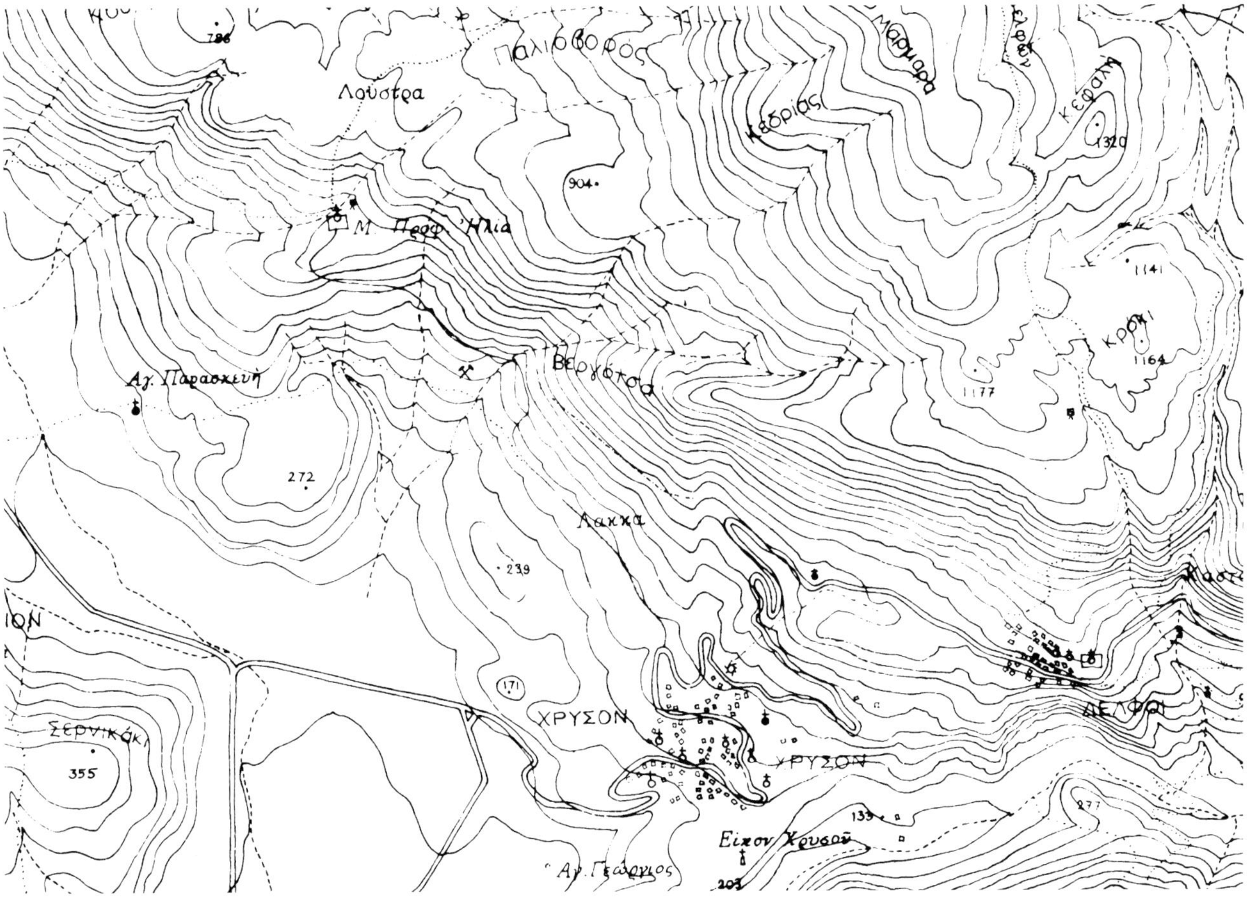

Fig. 10. Detail of a sketch map of the region around Delphi, re-drawn in 1966 by Algreen-Ussing, based on an older anonymous map found in the excavation house in Delphi. The quarry beneath the monastery of Profitis Elias has been marked, and a path connects it with the road to Delphi. Not included in the *Atlas*.

a historical monument and the settlement of later times; in this case, by a comparison of the topography in the excavated monument and the structure of the village that was built on top of this monument's abandoned stone circles and the transformation caused by the intervening culture layers (Fig. 7). It is a process that has been designated effective history and which today also includes the sanctuary's recreated attraction to the surrounding world.[14]

The second subject illustrates how the individual stone circles have been laid in proportion to each other on the steep mountain slope. That is, an analysis concerning the work processes that either led to a systematic construction of areas in all of the sanctuary based on a previously composed plan, or areas where the construction emerged as a more or less additive process of individual buildings without an overall plan.

An example of such an analysis is Erik Hansen's article "Les périboles du sanctuaire d`Apollon à Delphes",[15] which was studied during the course of the survey. In this article, Hansen examines whether an expansion of the sanctuary area took place, through a systematic shift of the east-, west- and south-ring wall of about 13 metres at the time that the great terrace and its temple were added to the sanctuary (Fig. 9). He writes:

"A new monumental sanctuary constructed according to a thorough well-defined plan was

[14] Gadamer, H-G., 1975 (1979). Rossi, A., 1982 (1989). Choay, F., 1992 (2001).

[15] Hansen, E., 1960

Fig. 11. In October 2008, Erik Hansen and I made a preliminary investigation of a possible track route from the quarry below the monastery of Profitis Elias to the temple site. In April 2010, several indications as cuttings in the bedrock, cart tracks and retaining-walls was measured and seems to be part of a transport route linking the quarry with the sanctuary. The photograph (author 2010) shows an example of these indications.

created with impressive terracing, in the place where the monuments had earlier been standing freely on the slope."

This distinction between the planned and the ad hoc-created public space contributed to the understanding of the conditions that a complex monument like the sanctuary was dependent on. The topological distinction that we make today in the analysis of the existing conurbations, in order to understand their architectonic character and significance in the urban structure, are of the exact same character, where one methodically separates the interpretation of the individual building from the interpretation that one ascribes to it in an urban framework.[16]

The third topic includes analyses of what one could call the catchment area. This means, for an example, a survey of the localities from which the building materials for the construction of the monuments were fetched and the transport routes that led all the way to the individual constructions in what, in antiquity, was a barely accessible construction site. There was no room for a topographic examination of this aspect in the atlas work, even though some sketches to this end were made.

This subject calls for new thematic maps

[16] Choay, F., 1992 (2001). Algreen-Ussing, G., 1997.

analysing the surrounding areas of the sanctuary with reference to the traces that must be left in the terrain, whether these traces are connected with the harbours of the sea transport or with localities in the area (Fig. 11). The character of this transport work without a doubt made demands on the size, form and weight of the building material, which for its part, set tectonic restrictions as to the construction and architecture of the monuments.[17]

[17] E.g. Bourguet, É., 1914; Amandry, P., 1981.

Bibliography

Algreen-Ussing, G., 1997
InterSAVE, International Survey of Architectural Values in the Environment, Ministry of Environment, Denmark.

Amandry, P., 1981
'Chronique delphique: Carrières', in *BCH* 105, 714-21.

Bommelaer, J.-F.,1992
'Postface', in *Delphes, Centenaire de la «Grande fouille» réalisée par L'École Française d'Athènes (1892-1903),* Leiden, 355-71.

Bourguet, É., 1914
Les ruines de Delphes, Paris.

Choay, F., 1992 (2001)
The invention of the historic monument, Cambridge, 138-48, 117-37.

Convert, H., 1897
'Plan du Village de Castri (Delphes)', *BCH* 21, pl. XIV-XV in Théophile Homolle, 'Topographie de Delphes', p. 256-320.

Dyggve, E., 1955
'Über Technik und Darstellung von Grabungen', in *Kunstchronik VIII,* Nürnberg, 144-7.

Gadamer, H.-G., 1975 (1988)
Truth and method, London, 305-41.

Hallager, E. & D. Mulliez (eds.) 2008
Une liaison française – 100 années de présence d' architects danois à l' École française d'Athènes, Athens.

Hansen, E., 1960
'Appendice, Les périboles du sanctuaire d`Apollon à Delphes', *BCH* 84, 423-33.

Hansen, E. & G. Algreen-Ussing (eds.), 1975
FD, Tome II, Topographie et Architecture. Sanctuaire d`Apollon, ATLAS, Paris.

Hansen, E., 2000
'Fra malerisk til analytisk – opmålingens historie i Danmark', in *Byggnadsuppmätning,* Sjömar, P. & E.Hansen & H.Ponnert & O.Storsletten (eds.), Riksantikvarieämbetet, 7-19.

Kejlbo, I., 1972
Historisk Kartografi, København, 50-1.

Lembech, M., 1961
Danske købstæder for to hundrede år siden og i dag, København.

Rasmussen, S.E., 1934
Moderne Arkitektur med særligt henblik på Danmark, København, 9.

Rossi, A., 1982 (1989)
The Architecture of the City, M.I.T.

Rousset, D., 2002
Le territoire de Delphes et la terre d`Apollon, Paris.

Tournaire, A., 1902
FD II, I, Paris.

Vrigny, Lacombe de, 1707
Travels through Denmark and some parts of Germany: by the way of journal in the retinue of the English envoy, in 1702. With a map of the isle of Huen; Done into English from the French original, London, 164-5.

Une pierre à Delphes*

Erik Hansen

Le relevé d'archicture est un dialogue avec l'objet que l'on désire étudier. Chaque observation couchée sur le papier donne occasion à des questions, qui amènent à d'autres observations et ainsi de suite. La figure 1 montre un architecte qui parle avec une pierre : un bloc de frise avec métope et triglyphe du temple d'Apollon à Delphes. L'architecte pèse 70 kg, la pierre 4 tonnes. Une telle pierre est difficile à remuer et lourde d'esprit. Il faut de la patience pour l'écouter, mais cela en vaut la peine : elle a une mémoire millénaire. La langue de communication est le relevé et les instruments de travail sont un double mètre et une équerre en fer, – ceux-là mêmes qu'emploient aujourd'hui les tailleurs de pierres. C'est tout.

Fig. 1. Un architecte et son objet (photo : P. Amandry 1980).

Sur la figure 2, on voit le résultat de cette conversation qui a duré quelques jours. La pierre a été dessinée sur chacun de ses six côtés à l'échelle 1/5. Ce ne sont pas des « images », mais des représentations schématiques de certaines observations, rendues par des symboles bien définis. Ainsi, la forme des cassures ne nous intéresse pas : elles sont montrées uniquement par une hachure uniforme qui dit qu'il n'y a aucune information à trouver ici. D'autre part, les traces des outils des tailleurs des pierres ont une grande importance et nous observons ici des symboles pour les ciseaux à pointe, à dents et le ciseau plat. Toutes les traces qui nous informent sur la manipulation et la connexion des blocs nous intéressent également : ainsi des crampons en forme de T qui relient les blocs entre eux et des goujons qui assurent la liaison entre les assises. À la face supérieure, nous observons une trace du joint de l'assise supérieure avec un trou de levier à côté qui permet de comprendre l'ordre de pose des blocs de cette assise, en l'occurrence de la gauche vers la droite. Ainsi nous pouvons suivre le travail des artisans et telle est bien notre intention.

Est-ce que ce dessin constitue pour autant une représentation objective de la pierre ? Non ! Il s'agit d'une sélection d'observations qui dépend de l'expérience de l'architecte et du but de son étude. Nous pouvons appeler cela un relevé « analytique ».

Cette méthode de travail que nous mettons aujourd'hui en œuvre est le résultat d'une évolution que nous pouvons suivre à travers les cent années illustrées par l'exposition que nous avons présentée ici et qui reflète aussi, dans ses grands traits, l'évolution

* Présenté d'abord au colloque «Von Handaufmass bis High Tech», 23-26 février 2000 à Cottbus et publié dans les actes du même colloque.

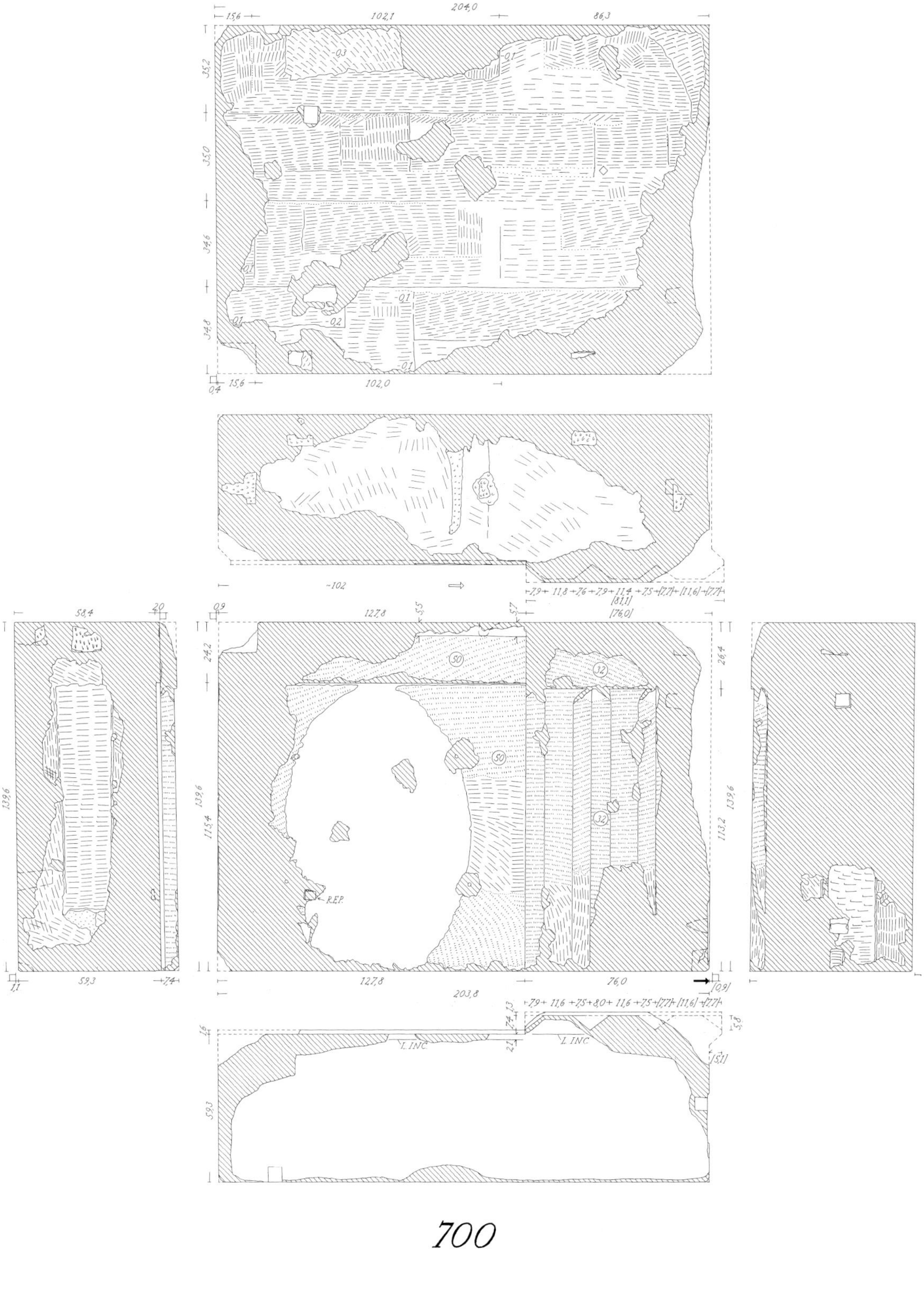

Fig. 2. Relevé d'un bloc de frise du temple d'Apollon du IVe siècle à Delphes avec métope et triglyphe, éch. 1/25. Les six faces sont montrées.

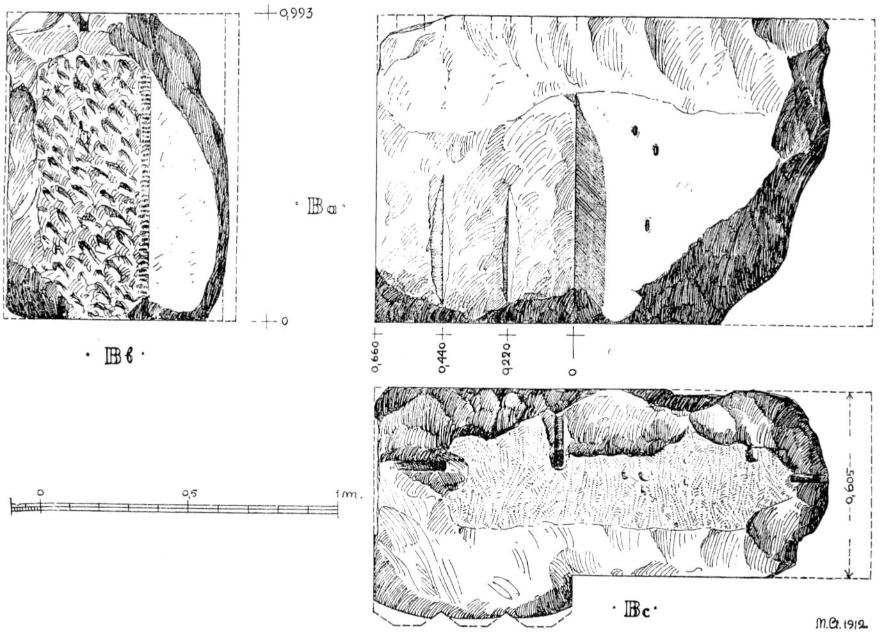

Fig. 3. Le temple d'Aléa Athéna à Tégée, IVe siècle. Bloc de frise avec triglyphe et métope. Relevé éch. 1/25, par M. Clemmensen (1913), pl. 59.

de l'architecture durant ce dernier siècle. Tentons de nous reporter un siècle en arrière. La figure 3 donne comme exemple le relevé d'un bloc de frise pareil à celui que nous venons de voir, dessiné en 1913 par M. Clemmensen, un des premiers architectes éminents qui ont travaillé pour l'École française au temple de Tégée dans le Péloponnèse. Pour M. Clemmensen et ses contemporains, formés aux styles historiques multipliant les détails, l'idéal était de rendre le plus fidèlement possible par dessin ce qu'ils voyaient, souvent à l'aide d'ombres, en rendant le caractère des matériaux, la surface des cassures et les autres traces des injures du temps à côté des traces laissées par les outils et les autres interventions sur la forme de la pierre. Mais avec l'évolution de l'architecture, d'abord vers le style néo-classique et ensuite le fonctionnalisme, disparaît aussi l'intérêt pour les détails et une certaine nudité domine alors les relevés des architectes. Les ombres et le rendu du caractère des surfaces ainsi que les traces des outils disparaissent des dessins, comme nous pouvons le constater également à travers cette exposition, – et l'on perd des informations. C'est sans doute Ejnar Dyggve, qui travaillait aux fouilles danoises de Kalydon, qui a remédié à cette perte d'information en définissant formellement une attitude scientifique dans le relevé architectural, en distinguant entre l'ancienne forme « pittoresque » et

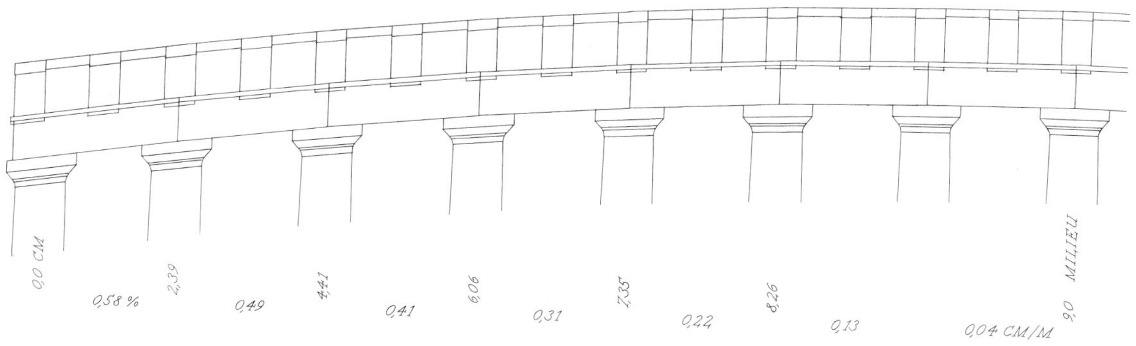

Fig. 4. Moitié gauche d'une façade avec courbure, croquis avec hauteurs exagérées; en bas l'inclinaison en % des blocs d'architrave (Parthénon, d'après F. C. Penrose [1846], pl. 12).

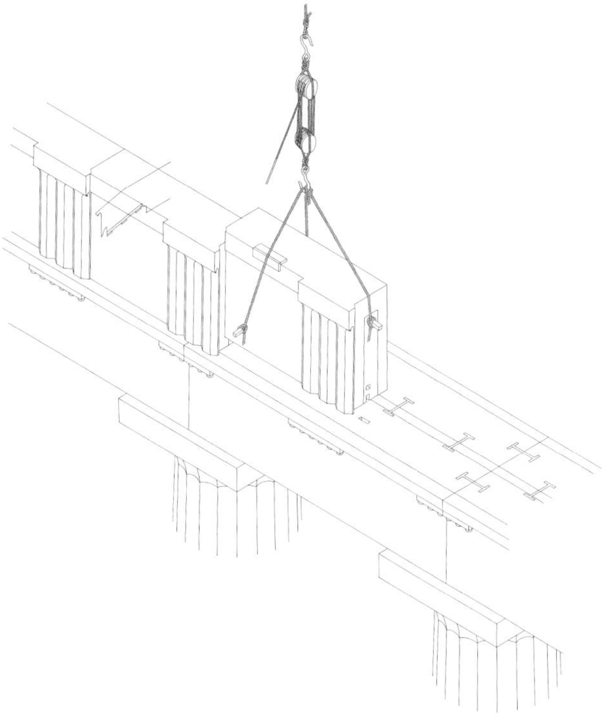

Fig. 5. Suspension du bloc lors de sa pose ; le travail avance de gauche à droite.

une nouvelle forme « stérile », celle qui a inspiré les travaux des dernières générations d'architectes, que nous préférons aujourd'hui appeler « analytique » et qui procède par une sélection de détails servant au but de l'étude.

Mais revenons maintenant à notre bloc de frise de Delphes (Fig. 2). Sur la face inférieure du bloc, on voit des restes de lignes incisées qui ont servi au tailleur des pierres pour la construction stéréométrique du bloc, ce qui permet une approche de la technique mise en œuvre. Dans cette étude, la notation très précise des mesures revêt également une grande importance pour nos réflexions sur l'architecture du monument. Par exemple, en regardant le côté gauche du bloc, nous mesurons avec l'équerre un écart de l'angle droit qui montre que la face antérieure a été inclinée de 2 cm vers l'arrière. Cela doit être l'une de ces finesses de l'architecture grecque qu'on appelle généralement « corrections optiques » et dont parle déjà Vitruve. Il y a une autre irrégularité qui se manifeste dans

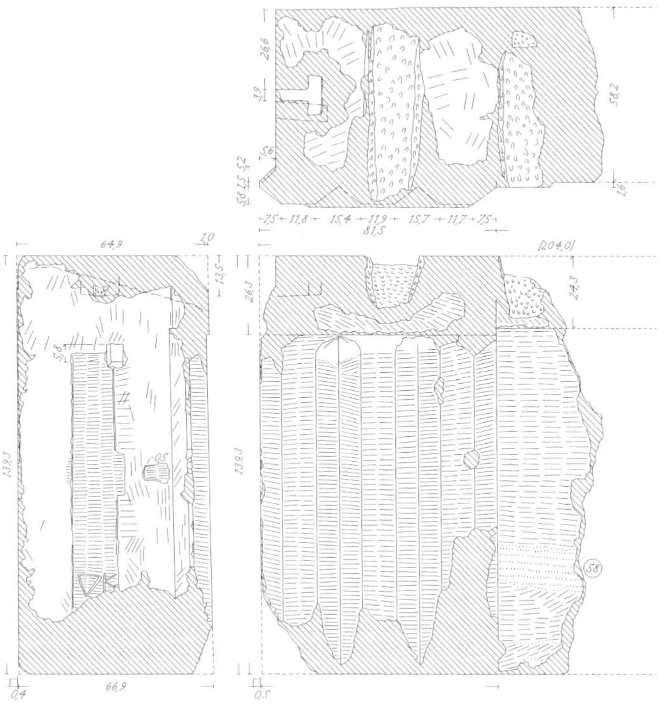

Fig. 6. Fragment de bloc de frise avec triglyphe à gauche (celui qui a permis la restitution axonométrique de la figure 7). À la face supérieure, on voit les entailles grossières destinées à recevoir les solives d'une toiture simple après l'incendie. Relevé 1/25.

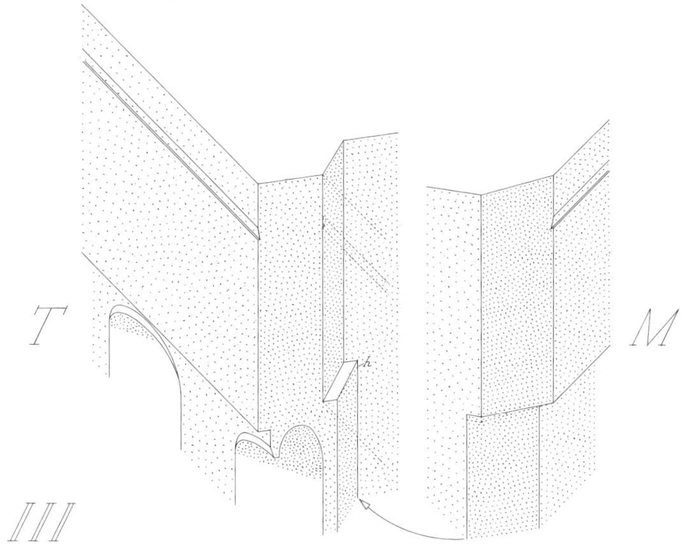

Fig. 7. Adaptation de deux blocs de frise : à gauche, la face de joint du côté triglyphe, qui a chevauché le joint côté métope du bloc voisin à droite (cf. fig. 5). Croquis axonométrique, éch. 1/8.

le fait que le joint gauche du bloc, ainsi que les côtés du triglyphe, ne sont pas perpendiculaires par rapport aux lits de pose et d'attente du bloc, mais présentent en haut un petit écart de 9 mm vers la droite. Comme on ne peut pas supposer que les triglyphes n'étaient pas verticaux, cela signifie que ce sont les lits de pose et d'attente du bloc qui n'étaient pas été strictement horizontaux. Il s'ensuit clairement que le temple a présenté une courbure, comme celle que nous connaissons bien pour Parthénon, dont nous montrons ici un dessin avec hauteurs exagérées, basé sur les mesures précises de Penrose en 1846 (Fig. 4). D'après l'inclinaison des lits de notre bloc, nous pouvons déduire qu'il a dû se trouver vers l'angle gauche de la façade. Un autre architecte danois travaillant à l'École, Hans Jakobsen, a trouvé un exemple similaire au temple d'Athéna en calcaire à Marmaria, contemporain du temple d'Apollon. Apparemment ce phénomène n'a donc pas été aussi rare qu'on pourrait le croire, même au IVe siècle avant J.-C.

Sur la face antérieure de la métope, on distingue le contour d'un bouclier qui était fixé par quatre clous et qui a ainsi protégé une partie de la surface originale, couverte d'une mince couche d'un stuc blanc très dur. Mais un violent incendie, qui a ravagé le temple à l'époque romaine, a nécessité un nettoyage des surfaces noircies par le feu, ce que l'on a fait par le passage grossier de ciseaux à lame et à dents autour de ce bouclier qui était resté en place.

Dans la partie supérieure de la face de joint droit, nous avons observé un petit trou carré, profond d'une vingtaine de centimètres. Il y en a un second identique dans la partie inférieure de la face postérieure et, en regardant bien, nous en distinguons un troisième à la face antérieure du bloc, sous le bouclier, mais ici soigneusement bouché et ensuite dissimulé sous le stuc. Rien à gauche. L'explication se trouve sur la figure 5 : ces trous étaient destinés au levage du bloc lors de la pose. Naturellement, l'attache des cordes a dû se faire sur trois points et la face de joint qui venait s'ajuster au bloc déjà posé devait être libre : on a donc procédé pour la pose de la gauche vers la droite. Le levage d'un poids de quatre tonnes sur une hauteur de dix mètres a nécessité une sapine importante. De fait,

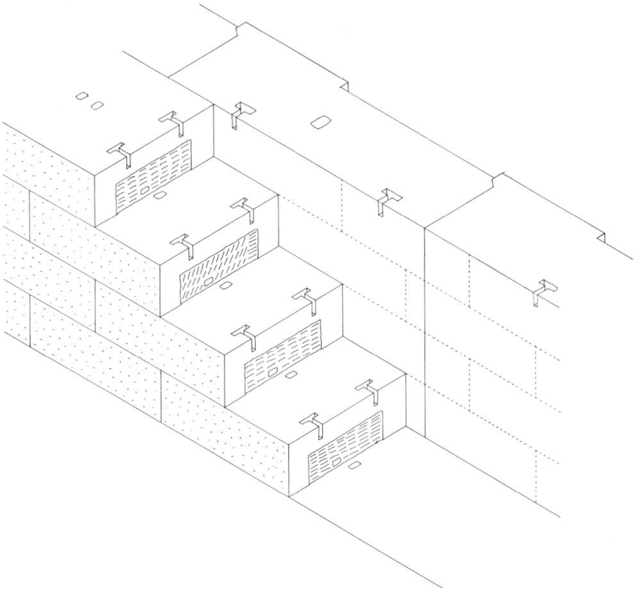

Fig. 8. La maçonnerie à la face postérieure de la frise, composée de quatre assises de blocs ayant la moitié de la longueur des blocs de frise. Restitution éch. 1/50. On remarque le décalage des joints par rapport à ceux de la frise.

on trouve le long des fondations de la façade Ouest du temple des trous carrés d'environ 30 x 30 cm destinés aux poteaux de cette construction, – un témoin rare des moyens techniques mis en œuvre lors de la construction d'un bâtiment de telles dimensions.

Évidemment, la pose de pareils blocs a constitué une opération délicate et il a fallu surtout éviter de heurter et d'épaufrer les angles fragiles des pierres : on leur a donné à cette fin une forme biseautée. Sur un autre bloc de triglyphe, dont la face de joint est mieux conservée (Fig. 6), nous voyons bien la forme précise de ces angles : elle implique aussi une saillie du triglyphe afin de couvrir le joint vertical de la métope du bloc voisin (Fig. 7). L'élaboration de ce point, qui a compris aussi les bandeaux en haut de la face antérieure, a demandé un solide sens de la stéréométrie chez le tailleur des pierres.

Pour compléter la largeur de l'assise, on a posé à l'arrière du bloc reproduit sur la figure 2 une maçonnerie en blocs plus petits et soigneusement adaptés à la face postérieure du bloc de frise. On voit, sur cette face, les légères traces laissées par le ciseau plat employé pour ajuster les différents blocs : pour bien les distinguer, il faut une lumière

Fig. 9. L'entablement du temple du IVe siècle avec notre bloc de frise dans son environnement originel. Restitution isométrique éch. 1/50. En haut du larmier, une moulure peinte avec des oves.

frisante ou, si l'on ne veut pas attendre que le soleil vienne dans la bonne position, il vaut mieux de travailler la nuit avec une lampe de poche, qui permet de diriger la lumière comme on le veut. C'est ainsi que, seul avec les pierres durant les nuits tièdes de l'été à Delphes on obtient, des révélations merveilleuses, pratiquant ainsi une « archéologie nocturne ». En soulignant à la craie les traces qu'on voit, on peut les transférer, le matin suivant, sur le papier, comme on le voit sur le relevé de la figure 2 (la craie s'enlève facilement avec de l'eau). Mais il faut encore les interpréter : c'est le résultat de cette interprétation que l'on voit figure 8. La maçonnerie de la contre-frise a consisté en quatre assises de blocs ayant la moitié de la longueur des blocs de frise et avec des joints décalés par rapport à ceux-ci. Nous en connaissons même le prix grâce à des fragments conservés des comptes de la construction du temple. Il y est question de livraisons de blocs provenant des carrières de Corinthe à 9 drachmes la pièce, ce qui doit correspondre à environ 180 drachmes avec le transport et la pose de chacun des ces blocs.

Enfin, la figure 9 montre notre bloc placé dans son contexte. Comme nous l'avons vu, la surface des murs était couverte d'un stuc blanc qui ressemblait à du marbre. Sur notre triglyphe, nous avons trouvé en outre des restes de bleu outre-mer et, en haut du larmier, il y avait une moulure avec des oves peintes en bleu, rouge et or. Quant aux boucliers, ils étaient dorés, ainsi que nous le savons par une source écrite. Ces boucliers étaient le butin pris sur les Perses après la bataille de Marathon : d'abord suspendus sur le temple des Alcméonides, ils furent transférés ensuite sur le nouveau temple du IVe siècle.

Mais aucune gloire n'est éternelle. Cinq siècles plus tard, comme nous l'avons déjà vu, le temple

Fig. 10. L'entablement après l'incendie d'environ 200 après J.-C, avec traces de réparations avec du béton appliqué sur une armature de branches, de cordes et de fer. – En haut les solives de la toiture secondaire.

fut ravagé par un incendie sans doute causé par la foudre qui a mis feu à la charpente. En tombant, les poutres ont brisé les angles des chapiteaux doriques, terminant ensuite sur le sol comme un grand bûcher, d'où les flammes ont endommagé les colonnes et les murs, arrivant même jusqu'à la face inférieure des architraves. Une inscription mentionne le consul romain Claudius Leonticus comme restaurateur du temple, vers 200 après J.-C. Nous voyons comment on s'y prit : avec du mortier retenu par une armature de branches, de cordes et de fer retenue par des piquets de bois fixés dans les surfaces abimées. Le larmier avait disparu avec la charpente et la belle toiture ainsi que le plafond à caissons furent remplacées par une construction plus simple, dont on a vu les traces sous forme d'entailles grossières creusées à la face supérieure de la frise (Fig. 6). Ainsi, le temple a survécu, tant mal que bien, jusqu'à son abandon ; puis, après une lente décrépitude, il a fini par être la proie des « chasseurs de trésors ».

On le voit, chaque pierre a son histoire à raconter. Comme nous avons identifié 850 fragments de ce temple avec Pierre Amandry, cela ferait presque des contes de 1001 nuits. Mais il suffit d'avoir raconté ici l'histoire de ce bloc de frise.

Bibliographie

Werfeling, U. & Heine, K. & Wulf, U. (red), 2000
Von Handaufmass bis High Tech. Bauaufnahmeverfahren in der historischen Bauforschung, Mainz.

Dugas, C. & Clemmensen, M., 1924
Le sanctuaire d'Aléa Athéna à Tégée, Paris.

Penrose, F. C., 1846
Principles of Athenian Architecture, London.

Étude et publication d'un matériel spécifique: Le cas des terres cuites architecturales de Delphes*

Christian Le Roy

En 1958, Karsten Rønnow a été invité par Georges Daux, alors directeur de l'École française d'Athènes, à se joindre à moi pour l'étude et la publication des terres cuites architecturales découvertes à Delphes pendant la « Grande Fouille » (1892-1902) et restées inédites. Notre collaboration a été relativement brève, moins d'un an, mais elle a été fructueuse, puisqu'elle a abouti à la publication d'un gros volume dans la collection des *Fouilles de Delphes*[1] qui, à en juger par les comptes rendus, a été favorablement accueillie[2].

Cette réussite est due, dans une large mesure, à Karsten Rønnow. Certes, il n'a été ni le premier architecte ni même le premier Danois à travailler sur les toits de la Grèce antique. À Delphes même, Kaj Gottlob a consacré beaucoup de temps au toit en marbre de la tholos de Marmaria[3]. En dehors de Delphes, Ejnar Dyggve a écrit des pages fondatrices sur les toits du Laphrion de Calydon[4]. Ces études sont précieuses, mais elles ne pouvaient servir exactement de modèles. Le matériel que nous devions étudier à Delphes avait des caractères propres demandant un traitement particulier. Quantitativement important – plus de 600 fragments de tuiles décorées, appartenant à au moins une cinquantaine de bâtiments – il était à la fois homogène par sa matière, la terre cuite, et par sa destination, les parties hautes des bâtiments, mais en même temps très diversifié par sa répartition dans le temps – de l'archaïsme à l'époque romaine – et dans l'espace, avec des centres de production allant de Corinthe à l'Italie méridionale en passant par Corcyre et la Sicile.

À ces problèmes liés à la nature du matériel, s'ajoutaient des difficultés dues aux conditions de leur découverte et aux insuffisances de l'inventaire[5]. Du reste, même si la fouille avait été menée comme on l'aurait fait au XXe siècle, seul un petit nombre de fragments aurait pu être rattaché avec certitude à un bâtiment repéré sur le terrain. L'histoire de Delphes a été marquée par de nombreuses catastrophes, naturelles ou causées par l'homme, de la destruction du temple des Alcméonides aux invasions barbares. Les tuiles en terre cuite sont un matériau relativement léger, facile à remployer ou à concasser pour être incorporé à un remblai. Cela a parfois entraîné la dispersion d'un bout à l'autre du sanctuaire de fragments appartenant au même toit[6].

* Je suis très reconnaissant à l'Institut archéologique danois d'Athènes et à l'École française d'Athènes, et spécialement leurs directeurs, les Professeurs Erik Hallager et Dominique Mulliez, de m'avoir offert la possibilité de présenter cette étude à Athènes et à Copenhague. Je remercie tout particulièrement les responsables de la planothèque et de la photothèque de l'École française d'Athènes qui ont assuré la numérisation des documents graphiques et photographiques ainsi que leur report sur CD.

1 Le Roy 1967.

2 Voir les comptes rendus de Heilmeyer, W.D., 1970,171-179 ; d'Agostino, B., 31-1,120-125 ; Phillips Jr, K.M., 1969, 382-383.

3 Gottlob, K., 1925.

4 Dyggve, E., 1948.

5 Le *Journal* de la « Grande fouille » ne mentionne qu'un petit nombre de terres cuites architecturales. De plus, les fragments recueillis étaient numérotés une fois par quinzaine ou une fois par mois. Par la suite, il y a eu d'autres tentatives de remise en ordre de lots de trouvailles non numérotées au moment de leur découverte, ainsi en 1913 (renseignements tirés d'une note inédite de P. de La Coste-Messelière).

6 Par exemple, le fragment S 150 du toit appartenant à un « Trésor » sicilien (toit 28) (Le Roy 1967, p. 70) a été trouvé près du trésor « étrusque » (Bommelaer, J.-Fr., 1991, n° 342) dans la partie Sud-Ouest du sanctuaire, et le fragment S 236 (Le Roy, Chr., 1967, 71) appartenant au même toit, a été trouvé dans le secteur de la Lesché de Cnide (Bommelaer, J.-Fr., 1991 n° 605) , soit dans l'angle diamétralement opposé du sanctuaire.

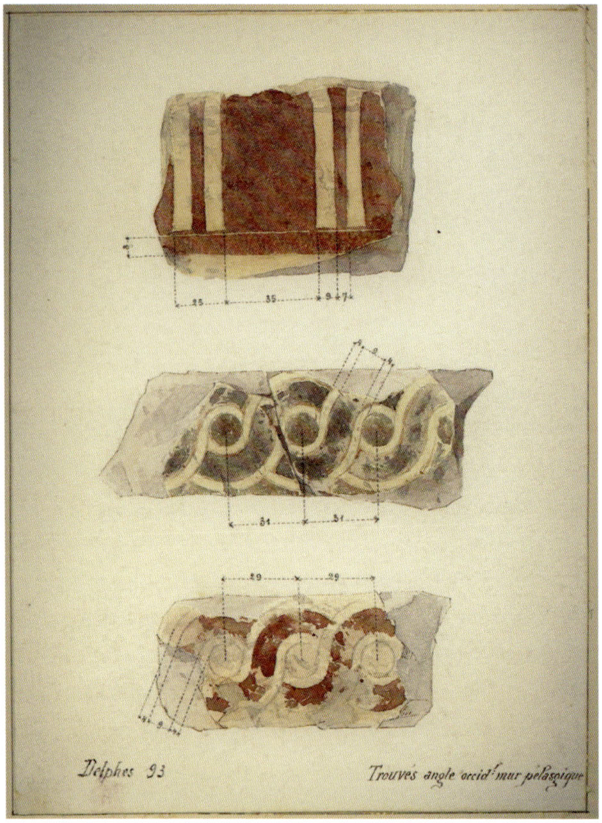

Fig. 1. Aquarelle d'A. Tournaire ; Delphes 1893. Archives EFA. « Trouvés angle occidental du mur pélasgique ». Au centre, R 30, série 8. Archives EFA. Inédit.

Tel était l'état du matériel pour lequel Karsten Rønnow et moi avions à élaborer nous-mêmes notre méthode. Les publications antérieures de terres cuites architecturales étaient en effet rarement satisfaisantes. Les très beaux volumes des fouilles d'Olympie[7] avaient vieilli et Alfred Mallwitz n'avait encore publié aucune de ses grandes études sur le sujet[8]. Ailleurs, on avait tendance à privilégier l'aspect décoratif de ces documents au détriment de leur rôle architectural. Il y avait heureusement quelques exceptions, dont la publication des terres cuites architecturales de l'Acropole d'Athènes par Ernst Buschor[9] en 1929.

À Delphes même, cependant, nous avions eu un prédécesseur : Albert Tournaire, architecte de la « Grande fouille » ayant travaillé à Delphes pendant les dernières années du XIXe siècle, avant de devenir l'un des principaux architectes français de

[7] Dörpfeld, W. & R. Bormann, 1896.

[8] La première étude où A. Mallwitz a étudié à fond un toit d'Olympie est sa publication, en 1964, de l'Atelier de Phidias : Mallwitz, A. & W. Schiering, 1964.

[9] Buschor E. 1929.

Fig. 2. Aquarelle d'A. Tournaire, Delphes 1894. S 25, toit 42. Archives EFA. Inédit.

son temps[10]. Il avait été sensible à la qualité de ces fragments, où il voyait sûrement un exemple de la polychromie des monuments grecs que l'on redécouvrait à cette époque[11]. Toutes les reconstructions graphiques d'un temple grec étaient rehaussées de couleurs variées, surtout dans les parties hautes. A. Tournaire avait ainsi réalisé, entre 1893 et 1896, d'après des fragments de terres cuites architecturales, quinze aquarelles aujourd'hui conservées dans les archives de l'École française d'Athènes[12]. Leur intérêt ne tient pas seulement à leur qualité esthétique et à leur exactitude, mais aussi aux renseignements qu'elles apportent sur des documents souvent négligés par les fouilleurs de l'époque

Ainsi, trois fragments ont été dessinés par Tournaire (Fig. 1) avec la date « Delphes 1893 » et l'indication : « trouvés angle occidental du mur pélasgique », c'est-à-dire, pour nous, le mur polygonal qui soutient la terrasse sur laquelle est bâti le temple d'Apollon. Nous savons que la construction de ce mur a entraîné la destruction de plusieurs bâtiments archaïques dont on n'a retrouvé que les fondations. Grâce à Tournaire, nous pouvons attribuer ces fragments à l'un de ces trésors du VIe siècle avant notre ère.

Même sans provenance, la date peut donner une indication utile : un fragment de sima de profil « corinthien » (Fig. 2) est classé, dans l'inventaire du Musée de Delphes, avec un lot attribué au temple en tuf d'Athéna à Marmaria. Or, il a été dessiné par Tournaire en 1894, date à laquelle la fouille de Marmaria était loin d'avoir débuté, puisqu'elle a été ouverte au début du XXe siècle. Grâce à Tournaire, nous savons donc que cette pièce appartenait à un monument qu'il faut chercher dans le sanctuaire d'Apollon.

Ces aquarelles furent présentées par Théophile Homolle à l'Académie des Inscriptions et Belles-Lettres le 7 juillet 1893. Le commentaire est laconique : « M. Homolle fait circuler les dessins de M. Tournaire d'après une série fort intéressante de terres cuites architecturales »[13]. Il n'y eut jamais de publication, seulement une mention élogieuse par Georges Daux dans l'introduction qu'il a rédigée pour le volume des *Fouilles de Delphes*. Cette petite collection reste donc aujourd'hui un document précieux, mais isolé. C'est une anthologie

Fig. 3. Toit 42, S 189 pl. 34. Photo EFA.

d'échantillons, sélectionnés pour leur qualité décorative, mais sans aucune tentative de constituer des séries et encore moins de reconstituer des toits.

Dans ces conditions, il nous est vite apparu, à Karsten Rønnow et à moi-même, qu'il fallait en premier lieu constituer des séries homogènes, que nous avons baptisées « toit » en associant dans un même ensemble, chaque fois que cela nous paraissait sûr ou même seulement vraisemblable, des simas, des antéfixes et des tuiles de rive. Ce faisant, nous avons fait un choix délibérément opposé aux critères de classement retenus par Van Buren et Shaw-Hill dans leurs publications respectives[14]. Puis, à l'intérieur de ces séries, il fallait mettre en évidence à la fois le côté « élément de la construction » et l'aspect « élément du décor », étant entendu que ces deux éléments sont indissociables : il est évident qu'une sima rampante richement ornée (Fig. 3), qui appartient au même toit que celle illustrée à la figure 2, est à la fois un élément

[10] Sur A. Tournaire à Delphes, voir Hellmann, M.-Chr. & Ph. Fraisse 1982, 290-291.

[11] Les recherches sur la polychromie dans l'architecture et la sculpture grecques se sont, ces dernières décennies, à ce point développées qu'on oublie parfois qu'elles ont commencé il y a près de deux siècles : voir Billot, M.-Fr., 1982.

[12] La liste des dessins de Tournaire n'a, à ma connaissance, pas été publiée. Je la donne ci-dessous en *Appendice*. On notera que certains des fragments dessinés n'ont pas été retrouvés en 1958.

[13] *CRAI* 1893, p. 212.

[14] Douglas Van Buren 1926 ; Thallon-Hill & King 1929.

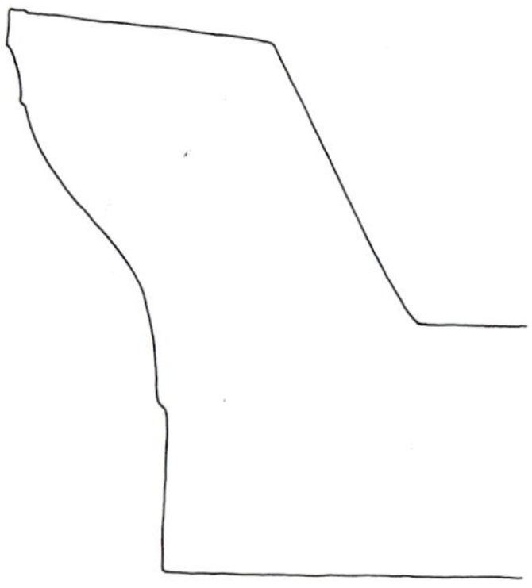

Fig. 4. Profil, Toit 81, S 91 + S 92. pl. 104. Archives EFA.

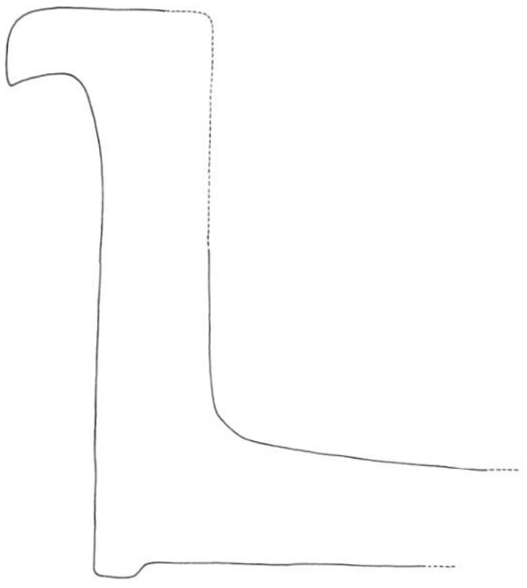

Fig. 5. Profil, Série 15, S 9 + S 207, pl. 99. Archives EFA.

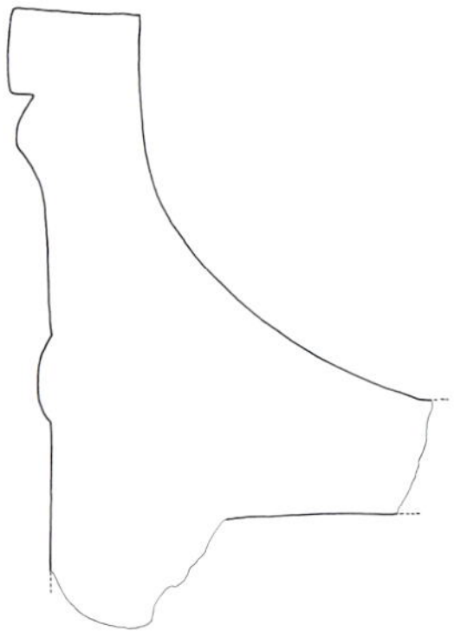

Fig. 6. Profil. Toit 27, G 6. pl. 100. Archives EFA.

fonctionnel relevant de l'architecture et un élément décoratif relevant de l'histoire de l'art. Mais il nous est clairement apparu qu'il fallait donner la priorité à l'architecture. C'est pourquoi le volume de la publication n'a pas paru dans la cinquième série des *Fouilles de Delphes*, consacrée aux « Petits objets » , mais dans la deuxième, intitulée *Topographie et architecture*[15].

Ces choix de méthode se retrouvent dans la distribution des planches graphiques de la publication. Un premier ensemble présente une série de profils de simas réalisés, non avec un conformateur (« template ») du type de celui qu'avait utilisé Lucy Shoe[16], mais avec un appareil, que nous avions baptisé « profilographe », inventé et construit par Erik Hansen (Fig. 4). Fondé sur le principe du pantographe, cet appareil permettait de suivre et de reproduire avec une grande exactitude les moulures en surplomb comme les cavets ou les becs de corbin, qu'il est difficile de suivre exactement avec un conformateur (Fig. 5 et 6).

La deuxième série de planches donne les relevés proprement dits réalisés par Karsten Rønnow. Il a choisi d'adopter des conventions proches de celles

[15] Sur le classement de la publication des *Fouilles de Delphes*, voir Bommelaer, J.-Fr., 1991, 9-12.

[16] Shoe, L.T., 1936, *passim*.

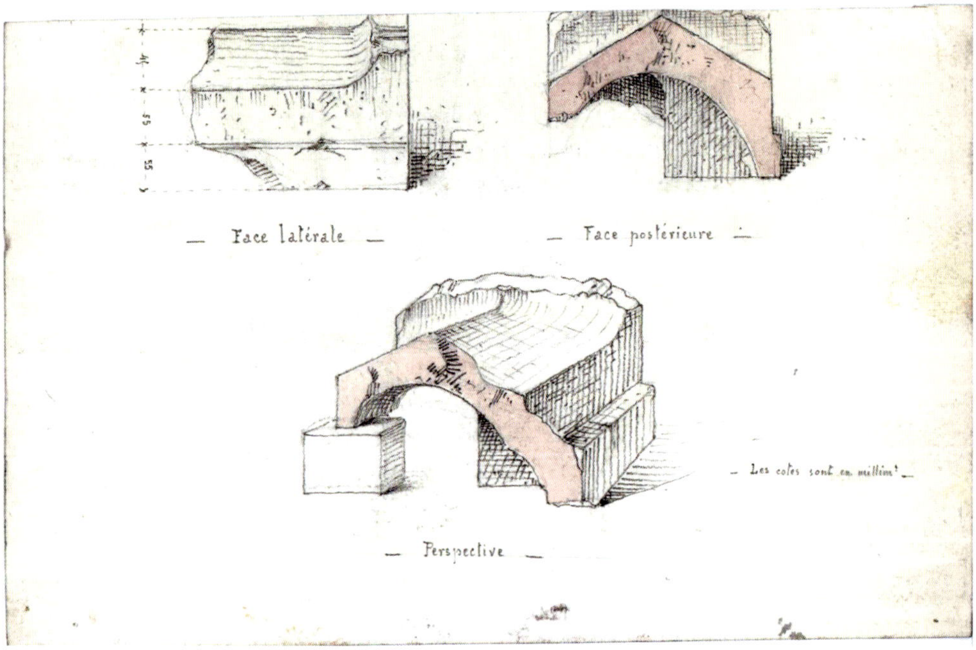

Fig 7. Couvre-joint, localisation inconnue, dessin anonyme. Archives EFA. Archives EFA. Inédit.

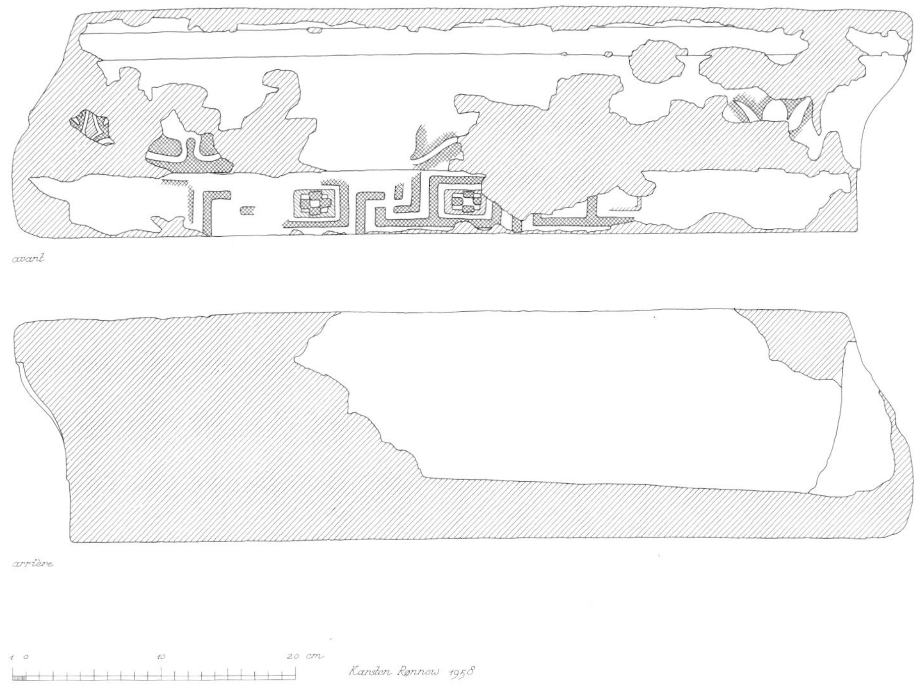

Fig. 8. Sima ; toit 81, S 94. pl. 114. Relevé K. Rønnow. Archives EFA.

utilisées par Erik Hansen. Le principe est de ne pas rechercher (sauf un cas évoqué ci-dessous) un réalisme d'imitation, pour lequel la photographie est le meilleur instrument. Je prendrai comme exemple de ce réalisme hérité du XIXe siècle un dessin tiré des archives de l'École française d'Athènes (Fig. 7), qui n'est pas de Tournaire (il n'est pas signé comme les précédents et ce n'est pas son graphisme) et qui représente bien ce que nous avons voulu éviter.

À l'opposé, Karsten Rønnow a cherché à mettre en évidence, par un système de conventions volontairement abstraites, l'expression des structures, des arêtes et des volumes. Le meilleur exemple est celui des cassures et des surfaces endommagées. Soit un fragment de sima présentant de nombreuses cassures (Fig. 8). Partant de l'idée qu'il est vain de prétendre reproduire exactement une surface brisée et qu'un raccord « Bruch am Bruch » ne sera jamais vérifié sur un dessin, mais seulement par le contact effectif de deux surfaces ou de leurs moulages, Karsten Rønnow a choisi, comme E. Hansen, de rendre les surfaces cassées par des hachures obliques exécutées à main levée. Cette technique, qui demande du temps et de l'habileté, a aujourd'hui été abandonnée au profit des trames exécutées par ordinateur. Sans vouloir jouer le *laudator temporis acti*, il faut cependant noter que la technique de la main levée a pour résultat de donner au dessin une sorte de vibration qui exclut toute sécheresse. Ces relevés sont certes austères, mais ils ne sont ni monotones ni ennuyeux. Dans le même esprit, les plans de coupe sont rendus par des hachures plus serrées, mais toujours à main levée (Fig. 9).

Ces choix, on l'aura compris, visent à traiter ces terres cuites comme de véritables fragments

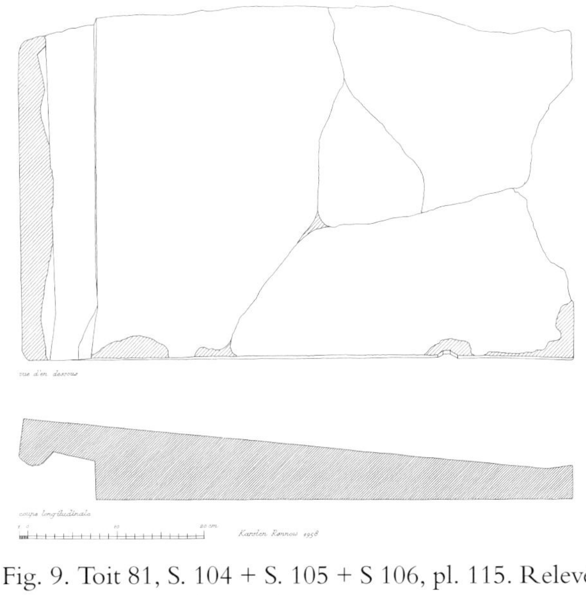

Fig. 9. Toit 81, S. 104 + S. 105 + S 106, pl. 115. Relevé K. Rønnow. Archives EFA.

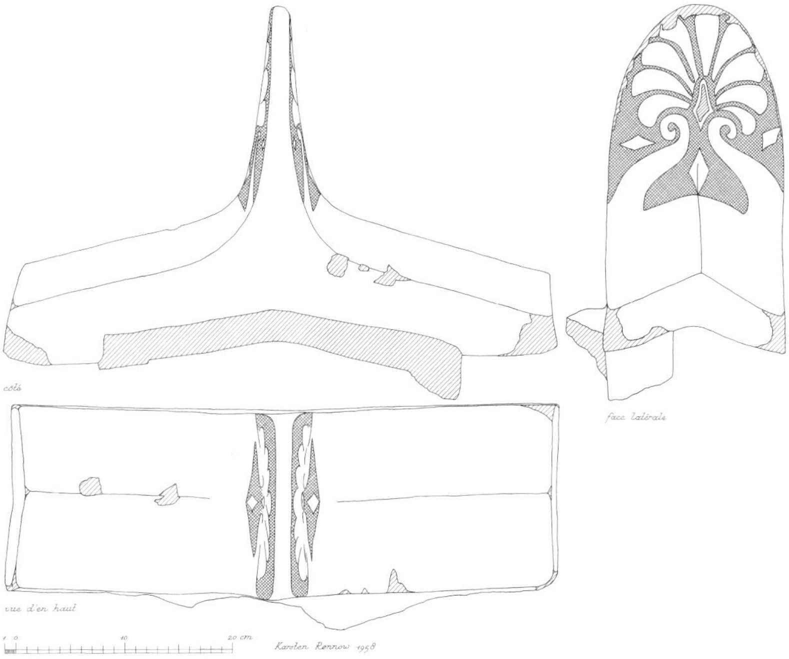

Fig. 10. Toit 81, F 10. pl. 117. Relevé K. Rønnow. Archives EFA.

Fig. 11. Toit 81, F 10, vue de face ; pl. 68. Photo EFA.

Fig. 12. Série 3, AR 1 , pl. 106. Relevé K. Rønnow. Archives EFA.

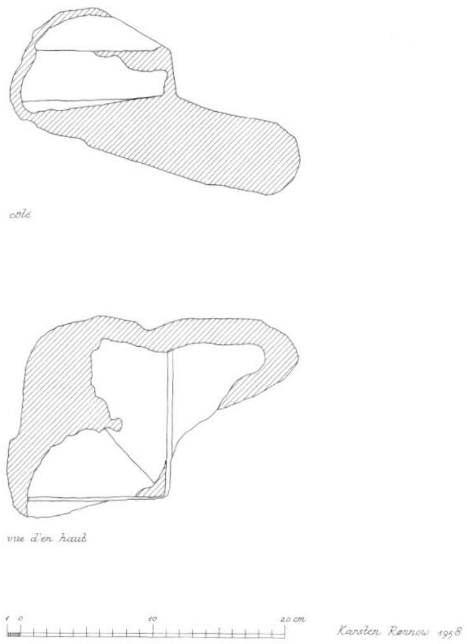

Fig. 14. Série 3, CJ 1 ; pl. 108. Relevé K. Rønnow. Archives EFA.

Fig. 13. Série 3, AR 1, revers. pl. 2. Photo EFA.

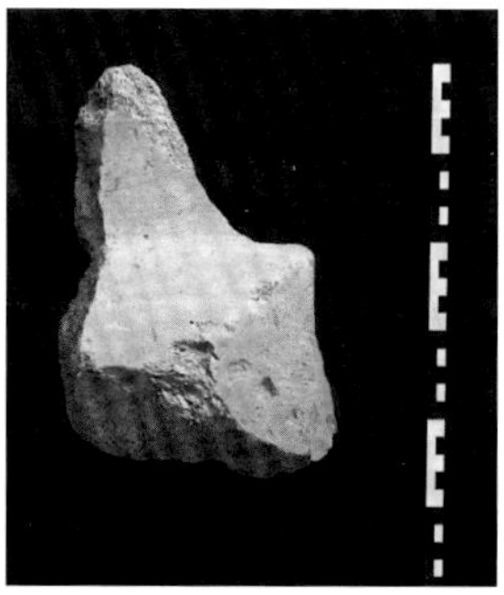

Fig. 15. Série 3, CJ.1, pl. 4. Photo EFA.

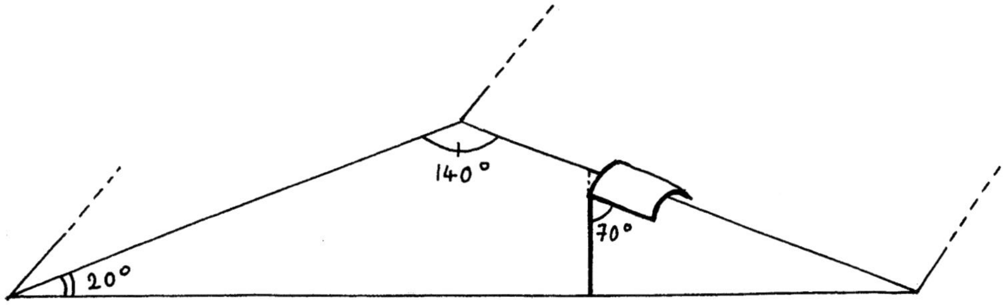

Fig. 17. Toit à croupe archaïque, essai de restitution, dessin de G. Le Roy, p. 22 fig. 1. Archives EFA.

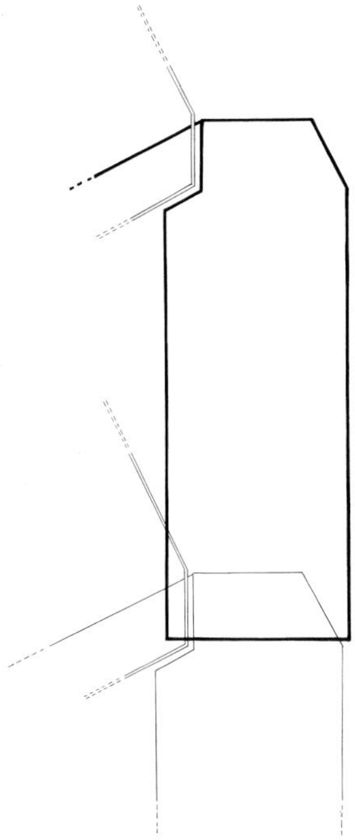
Fig. 16. Toit à croupe archaïque, essai de restitution ; dessin de G. Le Roy, p. 25 fig. 3. Archives EFA.

d'architecture, au même titre qu'un bloc de marbre ou de calcaire, et pas seulement comme le support d'un décor. Pour la même raison, Karsten Rønnow relève, quand il le juge utile, une pièce sous toutes ses faces : ainsi pour ce couvre-joint de faîte (Fig. 10 et 11). Ce parti implique que l'architecte, pour la vue d'en haut, dessine la pièce en projection, pour mettre en évidence les structures. Mais, en même temps, le rendu du motif décoratif se présente comme un signe, une sorte d'idéogramme : ce n'est pas du réalisme.

Une méthode se juge à ses résultats et l'on pourrait s'interroger sur l'utilité de traiter ces morceaux de tuiles comme des blocs du Trésor de Siphnos ou du temple d'Apollon. Je crois que notre publication le démontre et je n'en donnerai qu'un exemple. C'est sans aucun doute le regard à la fois austère et vigoureux de Karsten Rønnow qui nous a permis d'interpréter plusieurs fragments non décorés et, à Delphes au moins, sans parallèles : il s'agit d'un lot de grosses tuiles courbes à encoches, avec des surfaces évidées au revers et des amorces de tuiles plates ou concaves (Fig. 12 et 13) ou encore d'un fragment taillé à facettes qui est un élément de faîte (Fig. 14 et 15). C'est à partir d'une vingtaine de fragments analogues qu'on a pu restituer le schéma de montage d'un toit à croupe (« hip roof ») (Fig. 16 et 17). Dès lors il suffisait d'établir la comparaison avec les toits analogues découverts à Corinthe et à Isthmia[17] pour comprendre que nous avions là les restes d'un toit du VIIe siècle avant notre ère et très probablement celui du premier temple d'Apollon.

J'ai choisi cet exemple parce que c'est en quelque sorte de l'architecture à l'état pur, puisque les tuiles ne portent aucun décor. Mais c'est naturellement une exception puisque, dans la majorité des cas, les terres cuites portent un décor peint pour les simas ou moulé en léger relief et peint pour les antéfixes (Fig. 18). La publication de ces décors posait des problèmes, que rencontrent du reste toutes les publications où se rejoignent l'archéologie et l'histoire de l'art. Il n'était pas possible, pour des raisons financières évidentes, de publier en couleurs tous les fragments, ni même toutes les aquarelles de Tournaire. Aujourd'hui, avec la numérisation, nous aurions probablement un point de vue différent. Mais, en 1967, je n'ai pu donner qu'une seule planche en couleurs. En revanche, les planches photographiques en noir et blanc sont aussi nom-

[17] Connus grâce aux travaux de S.Weinberg, M.C. Roebuck et O. Broneer, dont les premiers résultats venaient d'être publiés : voir Roebuck, M.C., 1955, 112 ; Broneer, O., 1955, p. 112. La bibliographie n'a cessé de s'accumuler depuis lors. On se reportera commodément à la synthèse de Cooper, N., 1993, 12-18.

Fig. 18. « Antéfixe en terre cuite — Delphes 1896 » Dessin d'A. Tournaire. Objet non retrouvé en 1958. Archives EFA. Inédit.

Fig. 19. Toit 46, A 12 ; pl. 1 et 39. Photo EFA.

Fig. 20. Toit 46 (Marmaria, « temple en tuf » d'Athéna), A 12 ; pl. 109. Relevé K. Rønnow. Archives EFA.

Fig. 21. Toit 81, S 91 + S 92 ; pl. 116. Relevé K. Rønnow. Archives EFA.

breuses qu'on pouvait le souhaiter. Elles sont en grande majorité l'œuvre d'Émile Séraf. Plusieurs, dont celles des tuiles du premier temple d'Apollon dont il est question ci-dessus, sont de Karsten Rønnow. Pour les dessins, ce dernier a choisi de rendre les couleurs par des hachures ou des croisillons de types ou de densité variés se détachant sur le fond clair, comme on peut en juger par le relevé de cette antéfixe de la fin de l'archaïsme (Fig. 19 et 20).

Le traitement des décors peints posait un autre problème. Il s'agit la plupart du temps, pour les périodes classique et hellénistique, de frises de lotus et palmettes alternés. Si nous regardons le relevé d'une sima du début de l'époque hellénistique, proche de celle de la Stoa Sud de Corinthe (Fig. 21), on s'aperçoit que la frise de lotus et palmettes présente, dans le dessin, quelques irrégularités : ainsi, l'axe des palmettes n'est pas uniformément vertical. Karsten Rønnow a relevé la frise avec une exactitude rigoureuse, ce qui peut paraître en contradiction avec ce que j'ai écrit ci-dessus sur le recours aux symboles et à un graphisme abstrait. Mais, sur ce point comme sur d'autres, nous avons suivi l'exemple d'Erik Hansen. Ce dernier, lorsqu'il a abordé en

Fig. 22. Toit 56 (Lesché de Cnide), S 40 + S 175 ; pl. 1 et 46. Photo EFA.

Fig. 23. Toit 30 (Grande Grèce) ; pl. 122. Reconstitution du geison, dessin de G. Le Roy. Archives EFA.

1955, à Delphes, l'étude du trésor de Siphnos, a montré qu'on ne devait pas relever une frise d'oves en reproduisant mécaniquement le premier ove sur toute la longueur de la frise, mais que chaque ove devait être dessiné pour lui-même, aucun n'étant identique à ses voisins. Cette exigence concourt à faire parler le document et à ne rien omettre de ce qu'il peut nous apprendre. Lorsqu'on étudie un ornement, que ce soit une représentation abstraite ou figurative, il importe de reproduire avec exactitude l'écriture de l'artisan pour mieux la comprendre et pour éviter toute erreur d'interprétation. Dans le cas présent, la comparaison entre plusieurs toits est éclairante : ainsi, le décor de la sima de la Lesché de Cnide (Fig. 22) présente également des irrégularités dans le tracé des palmettes, dont l'axe dévie par rapport à la verticale. On peut faire des observations semblables sur d'autres fragments. Or, quelques archéologues avaient interprété ces variations comme le résultat d'une volonté de donner au décor un mouvement latent (*lanthanousa kinêsis*), bref un raffinement optique de plus dans l'art des architectes grecs[18]. Je crois avoir montré que, au moins pour les terres cuites architecturales de Delphes, cette théorie est contredite par les faits.

[18] Cf. Rhomaios, K., 1951, *passim*. Stucchi S., 1952-54, 24-36.

Fig. 24. Toit 30 (Grande Grèce), G 19. Aquarelle d'A. Tournaire, « Delphes, Novembre 93 ». Archives EFA.

Fig. 25. Toit 45 (Marmaria, temple d'Athéna dit « temple en tuf »). Sima S 28 + S 29 + S 211 ; pl. 38. Photo EFA.

Fig. 26. Toit 45 (Marmaria, temple d'Athéna dit « temple en tuf »), reconstitution de la sima. Dessin de G. Le Roy. Pl. 124. Archives EFA. Cf. J.-Fr. Bommelaer 1991, p. 253, fig. 115.

En réalité, la mise en série des simas et antéfixes de Delphes qui présentent ce type d'irrégularités montre que ces variations sont de caractère aléatoire : elles ne suivent aucun ordre, elles ne sont pas le résultat d'une volonté délibérée de l'artisan. J'ai pu en faire la démonstration en m'appuyant à la fois sur les photos d'Émile Séraf et les relevés de Karsten Rønnow.

Ces remarques nous conduisent à poser un autre problème, que je voudrais évoquer en conclusion : il s'agit des restitutions graphiques. Après la publication, on m'a parfois reproché d'avoir été, sur ce point, plutôt timoré. Et il est vrai qu'on ne trouve pas, dans ce livre, ces toits entièrement restitués qui font le bonheur des auteurs de manuels d'architecture. La raison est que je n'avais pas de données sûres pour plusieurs facteurs déterminants, tels que la pente d'un toit, la longueur des rampants ou celle des longs côtés. En revanche, nous avions, pour un bon nombre de toits, suffisamment de fragments, même non raccordés entre eux, pour pouvoir restituer leur décor. Avant son retour au Danemark, Karsten Rønnow a eu le temps de dessiner la restitution de deux simas, une tuile faîtière, une tuile de rive avec son antéfixe et une tuile plate[19]. Après son départ, Gisèle Le Roy a réalisé à Delphes les dessins restitués de 8 simas, 14 antéfixes, 3 plaques de geison et une tuile de rive[20]. En ce qui concerne le rendu des motifs et des couleurs, nous avons utilisé des conventions proches de celles adoptées pour les relevés : un jeu contrasté de hachures et de croisillons se détachant sur

Fig. 27. Toit 56 (Leschè de Cnide). Restitution de la sima. Dessin de G. Le Roy. Pl. 126. Archives EFA. Cf. J.-Fr. Bommelaer 1991, p. 253 fig. 115.

[19] Le Roy, Chr., 1967, planches 130-134

[20] *Ibid.*, planches 118-129.

un fond clair a permis de conserver l'essentiel de l'expressivité graphique, comme le montre la restitution d'un revêtement de *geison* venu de l'Italie du Sud (Fig. 23), que l'on comparera avec l'aquarelle réalisée par Tournaire d'après le fragment le mieux conservé de ce revêtement (Fig. 24).

Autre problème lié au décor des simas : fallait-il reproduire le décor tel que le spectateur le voit, en tenant compte du profil de la sima, et donc en projection ? Nous l'avons tenté pour la sima de profil « corinthien » qui couronnait le temple en tuf d'Athéna à Marmaria, mais le résultat ne nous pas semblé très heureux (fig. 25-26). Finalement, il nous a paru plus conforme à l'esprit de la publication de ne pas rechercher le réalisme, mais de donner une restitution développée du profil et du motif décoratif, qui ne fait pas double emploi avec la photographie ou avec le relevé et fait mieux ressortir le graphisme et la lisibilité du décor, comme c'est le cas ici pour la sima de la Lesché de Cnide (Fig. 22 et 27). Ainsi les restitutions s'inscrivent, quoiqu'elles poursuivent un objectif différent, dans la même logique que les relevés.

C'est à vous de juger si nous avons atteint notre but . Ce dont je suis sûr, c'est que cela a été pour moi un privilège que de pouvoir, pendant plusieurs mois, partager l'acuité du regard et la qualité de la réflexion de Karsten Rønnow. J'ai beaucoup appris, et, cinquante ans après, ma reconnaissance est intacte.

Appendice

Concordance des fragments de terres cuites architecturales dessinés par A. Tournaire

N° Photothèque EFA	Date	N° dans la publication
N 122.01	1893	a) en haut, non retrouvé b) au centre, R 30, série 8 c) en bas, non retrouvé, série 8
N. 122. 02	1893	A 37, toit 14
N. 122. 03	1894	S 207, série 15 ; S 173, toit 58
N. 122. 04	1894	G 10, G11, G12, G 34, toit 27
N. 122. 05	1893	G. 19, toit 30
N. 122. 06	1896	A. 189, toit 30
N. 122. 07	1896	A.134 série 104 + A 11 série 36
N. 122. 08	1894	S 25 toit 42
N. 122. 09	1896	AC 3 série 38 + non retrouvé
N. 122. 10	1893	S 64 toit 70
N. 122. 11	1896	A 68, toit 81 + non retrouvé, série 64
N. 122. 12	1896	Toit 82
N. 122. 13	1893	non retrouvé ; toit 84
N. 122. 14	1893	S. 180, série 49
N. 122. 15	1893	R 33, série 82

Bibliographie

Billot, M. Fr., 1982
Recherches aux XVIIIe et XIXe siècles sur la polychromie de l'architecture grecque, in Hellmann (M.-Chr.) et Ph. Fraisse (dir.) 1982, 61-125.

Bommelaer, J.Fr. & D. Laroche, 1991
École française d'Athènes, Sites et monuments 7, *Guide de Delphes, Le site,* Athènes – Paris.

Broneer, O., 1955
« Excavations at Isthmia », *Hesperia* 24, 112.

Broneer, O., 1962
« Excavations at Isthmia », *Hesperia* 31, 21-22.

Buschor, E., 1929
Die Tondächer der Akropolis, Berlin.

Charbonneaux, J, & K. Gottlob, 1925
Fouilles de Delphes II, *Topographie et architecture, Le sanctuaire d'Athéna Pronaia, La Tholos,* Paris.

CRAI
Comptes rendus des séances de l'Académie des Inscriptions et Belles-Lettres, Paris

Douglas Van Buren, E., 1926
Greek fictile revetments in the archaic period, London.

D'Agostino, B., 1969
Recensione di Le Roy & *alii* 1967, *Archeologia Classica* 21 – 1, 120-125.

Dörpfeld, W. & R. Bormann, 1896
Die Baudenkmäler, E. Curtius & F. Adler, *Olympia, Die Ergebnisse der Ausgrabungen*, Berlin

Dyggve, E. & F. Poulsen, 1948
Das Laphrion, Der Tempelbezirk von Kalydon, Copenhagen.

Heilmeyer, W. D., 1970
Rezension Le Roy & *alii* 1967, *Gnomon* 42, 171-179.

Hellmann, M. Chr. & Ph. Fraisse (eds.), 1982
Paris – Rome – Athènes, Paris.
Le Roy, C., K. Rønnow, G. Le Roy & J. Ducat, 1967
Fouilles de Delphes II, *Topographie et architecture, Les terres cuites architecturales. La sculpture décorative en terre cuite*, Paris.

Mallwitz, A. & W. Schiering, 1964
Die Werkstatt des Pheidias in Olympia (Olympische Forschungen 5), Berlin.

Phillips, K.M., Jr., 1969
Recension of Le Roy *et al.*, 1967, *AJA* 73, 382-383.

Rhomaios, K., 1951
Keramoi tês Kalydônos, Athens.

Roebuck, M.C., 1955
« Excavations at Corinth », *AJA* 43, 592.

Shoe, L.T., 1936
Profiles of Greek mouldings, Harvard, Cambridge Mass.

Stucchi, S., 1952-54
« Nota introuttiva sullencorrezioni ottiche », *Annuario* 30-32, 24-36.

Thallon-Hill, I. & L. Shaw King, 1929
Decorated architectural terracottas, Corinth 4, 1, Harvard, Cambridge, Mass.

Ce que j'ai appris au contact des architectes danois*

Jean-François Bommelaer

Pour être admis à l'École Française d'Athènes, dont j'ai été membre de 1966 à 1970, je m'étais familiarisé avec l'architecture antique dans les manuels courants, de langue anglaise, mais surtout dans deux ouvrages écrits en français. Le premier, qui datait de plus de quarante ans, était la publication du temple de Tégée[1] : s'il reste exemplaire aujourd'hui encore, c'est grâce à l'excellente qualité des relevés et restitutions des architectes danois Sven Risom et Mogens Clemmensen (Fig. 14 et 15a), ainsi qu'à la bonne collaboration entre ceux-ci et l'archéologue. Le deuxième était la thèse, alors toute récente, de Georges Roux sur l'architecture de l'Argolide[2], qui montrait en particulier à quel point la connaissance des inscriptions grecques et celle de l'architecture antique se confortent mutuellement; elle présentait en outre l'avantage de comporter plusieurs dessins de la main d'Erik Hansen.

Un agenda bien chargé m'attendait lorsque je suis arrivé à l'École à la fin de novembre 1966 : à Delphes, «nettoyage» d'un monument de Delphes pour en permettre un relevé complet; à Argos, classement d'une abondante céramique trouvée au cours de l'année et qui encombrait les réserves du musée; ces deux opérations devaient être menées à bien avant la campagne de fouille à laquelle je participerais au printemps suivant, à Argos aussi. Dans deux cas sur trois, j'allais avoir affaire à de jeunes Danois, diplômés ou étudiants en architecture. Ici, sans respecter strictement la chronologie, je ne dirai que quelques mots de l'expérience argienne de cette campagne, pour parler ensuite plus longuement de l'expérience delphique commencée avant et continuée après, de ses acquis ainsi que de certaines erreurs qui ont été commises au cours de cette année 1966-7 et corrigées ensuite, et enfin j'évoquerai ma collaboration avec Erik Hansen, qui s'est développée surtout au cours de ces dernières années.

Argos (printemps 1967)

Les fouilles françaises d'Argos venaient de reprendre après une longue interruption. Au printemps de 1967, on ouvrit trois chantiers ; je ne parlerai que de deux d'entre eux. L'un était à l'Agora, où une demande de permis de construire rendait urgente l'intervention des archéologues. Yvon Garlan, Haiganuch Sarian et Jean-Pierre Sodini fouillèrent au ras d'une maison que sa propriétaire aurait voulu agrandir, trouvèrent un monument recouvert par cette maison et, sous ce monument, un tronçon du grand égout de la ville antique, dont le fond était situé à plus de 5 mètres en dessous du niveau du sol moderne. Søren Blaabjerg arriva un beau jour et fit pratiquement tout seul le relevé détaillé dont on a publié une copie simplifiée dans la chronique du *BCH* de l'année suivante[3]. Le caractère acrobatique de l'exercice, réalisé en sabots et sans aucune protection, a laissé aux spectateurs un souvenir émerveillé.

Le deuxième chantier avait été ouvert au Sud de l'Odéon. Le site, placé juste au pied de la colline qu'on appelle la Larissa, est constamment menacé par un fort ruissellement des eaux de pluie. De fait,

---

* La communication que je présente ici diffère un peu de celle que Dominique Mulliez et Christian Le Roy m'ont fait l'amitié de lire à ma place aux deux sessions du Séminaire, parce que, dans cette première version, j'avais multiplié les figures dont certaines n'étaient pas publiables en l'état.

[1] Voir Dugas, E., J. Berchmans & M. Clemmensen 1924.

[2] Voir Roux, G., 1961.

[3] Voir *BCH* 92 (1968), face à 1001.

Fig. 1. Argos, Aphrodision, plan partiel de la fouille de 1967, éch. 1/100 (S. Blaabjerg, *BCH* 92 (1968), face à 1002, © EFA).

ce ruissellement avait, à plusieurs reprises, renversé des murs de terrasses et emporté une partie des sédiments archéologiques. Les gens qui avaient reconstruit à plusieurs reprises avaient mélangé les vestiges d'époques différentes (de l'Helladique Moyen au Byzantin), en fondant les nouveaux murs parfois aussi profondément que les anciens, mais selon des orientations diverses. Comme nous ne voulions rien détruire avant d'avoir attribué un statut à chaque structure, nous avons demandé à Søren de faire tout figurer sur un même plan, avec des traits d'une seule épaisseur. Le résultat était d'une précision extrême, mais en même temps d'une complexité qui, bien entendu, rendait ce plan incompréhensible.

Le dessin publié dans la même chronique, qui comporte des traits d'épaisseurs différentes, résulte d'une interprétation élaborée par Francis Croissant et moi-même au cours de l'automne ou de l'hiver suivant (Fig. 1)[4]. Il nous avait fallu beaucoup plus de temps que le séjour de Søren n'avait duré. Celui-ci n'avait donc fourni qu'une donnée brute avant de nous quitter pour rejoindre les fouilleurs de Délos. Mais ce n'était absolument pas de sa faute : le système de management utilisé alors par l'École française privait les fouilleurs d'une partie de ce que l'œil et la formation d'un architecte auraient

[4] Voir *ibid.*, 1021-39, notamment fig. 2.

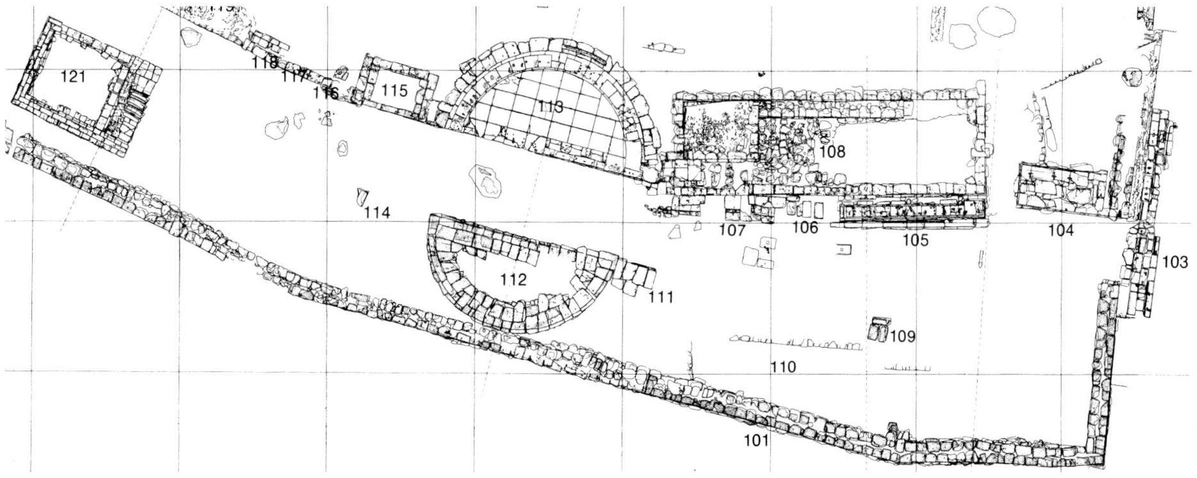

Fig. 2. Delphes, sanctaire d'Apollon, plan du secteur Sud en 1967, éch. 1/500 (Hansen, E., G. Algreen-Ussing & *alii*, 1975, *FD, Atlas*, pl. III, © EFA).

pu leur apporter en matière d'observation et de raisonnement.

Delphes, sanctuaire d'Apollon, secteur Sud (1966-1967)

La mission

Georges Daux, directeur de l'École, m'avait expédié à Delphes dès l'hiver 1966-7 pour aider une équipe de quatre Danois (un architecte et trois étudiants en architecture)[5], qui travaillaient déjà dans le secteur Sud du sanctuaire d'Apollon. Cette formule n'était pas courante : on a vu que, d'habitude, c'étaient les architectes qui travaillaient pour les archéologues. Mais les études delphiques traversaient alors une crise, parce que Georges Roux venait de mettre en cause, entre autres doctrines qu'on croyait établies, celle qui concernait le monument dit des *navarques*[6]. Sachant, d'après Plutarque et Pausanias, que ce monument célébrait la victoire d'Aigos Potamoi remportée en 405 av. J.-C. par le Lacédémonien Lysandre (en prélude à la prise d'Athènes en 404) et qu'il se trouvait près de l'entrée Sud-Est du sanctuaire, on en replaçait généralement les nombreuses statues de bronze entre les murs de la niche de brèche 108 (Fig. 2 et 3), qu'on restituait comme un portique. G. Roux soutenait qu'il y avait là trois erreurs : à son avis, 1° les *navarques* figuraient sur une base située de l'autre côté de la voie, de l'entrée jusqu'aux blocs numérotés 109, 2° la niche était nettement plus récente, 3° elle ne comportait pas de portique...

Pour en avoir le cœur net, G. Daux avait chargé les quatre Danois de faire un relevé complet de la niche (au $1/20^{e}$), des dalles de calcaire qu'on pouvait lui attribuer et des blocs des plinthes des statues, eux aussi en calcaire (au $1/5^{e}$). Avaient-ils d'autres instructions ? Cela ne me regardait pas, m'a dit Philippe Bruneau, le secrétaire général de l'École qui m'avait conduit sur place; traiter le dossier revenait à Jean Bousquet, mais, comme celui-ci était retenu à Rennes par son enseignement, j'étais chargé de nettoyer les fondations de la niche 108 pour en permettre le relevé : je ne devais regarder l'architecture ni de ce monument ni de ses voisins, qui étaient tous « en mains »... À défaut de l'architecture, j'ai regardé les « architectes » tout en

[5] Jörn Damsgaard, Eva Gleerup-Andersen, Henriette Howalt (à mi-temps) et Erik Olsen (le seul des quatre qui fût déjà diplômé, m'ont-ils dit alors). Je me permets de rectifier deux indications dans Hallager, E. & D. Mulliez (éd.) 2008, 88 : ils étaient bien quatre (et non deux), et l'épisode date non pas de 1964, mais de 1966-7, période pendant laquelle Gregers Algreen-Ussing et Annelise Bramsnæs contrôlaient et copiaient à l'encre le relevé général du sanctuaire d'Apollon, auquel les quatre susnommés avaient participé.

[6] Roux, G., 1963, 16-36. Sur le travail de ces années, voir *BCH* 92 (1968), 1047-60; sur le problème des *navarques,* Bommelaer, J.-Fr., 1981.

Fig. 3. Delphes, portique 108 : vue générale de face après la remise en place du stylobate (cliché JFB, 1970).

Fig. 4. *Idem* : angle Sud-Est reconstruit, à l'exception du stylobate (cliché JFB, 1967).

accomplissant ma tâche à ma façon[7]. Je les ai vus faire non seulement les relevés susdits, mais aussi un catalogue de tous les blocs de brèche «errants», qui n'avaient jamais intéressé personne. Ils proposaient pour chacun une attribution en utilisant comme critère, m'ont-ils dit, le travail antique tel que ses traces le faisaient connaître. Donc une observation exacte et l'exhaustivité étaient leurs maîtres mots.

Les résultats de l'équipe danoise

J'ai d'autant moins oublié cette leçon que l'équipe est parvenue à des résultats très appréciables. Je cite tout de suite le plus visible, bien qu'il soit intervenu plus tard et qu'il concerne un autre monument : c'est la remise en ordre des blocs (en calcaire de «Saint Élie») de la façade de l'hémicycle voisin 113, dit des *Rois d'Argos*, dont personne depuis 70 ans ne s'était avisé qu'elle avait été mal remontée au moment de la « grande fouille »[8]. Autre preuve de virtuosité, le rapprochement de fragments disjoints. J'ai publié ailleurs les avancées que de tels raccords avaient fait faire à la connaissance du monument des *navarques*[9]. On voit ici (Fig. 5) comment certaines dalles de la niche 108 ont été recomposées, notamment à partir de petits fragments que mon « nettoyage » avait extraits d'un sol bétonné de date tardive. Mais la reconstruction des assises 4, 5, 6 et 7A (première assise plate) de l'angle Sud-Est de la niche 108 (Fig. 4) et la remise en place de quelques blocs dans le mur de fond, peut-être moins spectaculaires, me paraissent mériter des éloges encore plus grands, parce que ces blocs de brèche, initialement dispersés dans les broussailles hors du sanctuaire, étaient parfois usés et d'autant

[7] J'avais fouillé en France sous la direction de Paul Courbin.
[8] Voir *BCH* 92 (1968), 1053, fig. 7-8
[9] Voir Bommelaer, J.-Fr. 1971.

Fig. 5. Delphes : dalles ordinaires du portique 108 recomposées (cliché JFB, 1967).

plus difficiles à replacer que plusieurs d'entre eux ne comportent pas de cuvettes de crampons : à leur sujet, le catalogage et l'observation ont assurément fonctionné de pair.

Certaines des opérations évoquées ci-dessus ont eu lieu en mon absence. C'était normal dans la situation initiale. Ce l'était moins depuis ce jour du printemps 1967 où J. Bousquet, venu de France, m'a confié la responsabilité du dossier : ce transfert s'est produit à la fin de son séjour en Grèce, c'est-à-dire au moment même où le programme de l'École m'envoyait fouiller à Argos jusqu'au début de l'été[10]. Les architectes s'étaient donc retrouvés seuls du fait d'une nouvelle erreur de management. L'été venu, quand je suis retourné à Delphes, ils étaient en pleine activité de reconstruction après avoir groupé beaucoup de blocs en face de la niche. Ils se sentaient alors propriétaires des résultats obtenus au point de refuser d'en discuter et même de les expliquer : «les pierres montrent d'elles-mêmes à quoi elles ont servi», m'a répondu E. Olsen. Il était clair qu'ils achevaient une phase du travail concernant les monuments 108 et 109, tout en s'occupant de l'hémicycle 113 déjà cité et d'autres offrandes encore. J'ignore s'ils avaient commencé à préparer une phase ultérieure. En tout cas, si le dossier qu'ils m'ont remis lorsqu'ils ont quitté Delphes avant la fin de l'été contenait bien les relevés (au crayon) des blocs de calcaire de l'état initial de la niche 108 et de ce qu'ils avaient reconstruit, il ne comportait absolument rien au sujet d'une telle phase[11].

La recherche ultérieure sur le portique 108

Une fois en possession de leurs dessins, je n'ai pas mis longtemps à apprendre ce que les quatre architectes avaient découvert et ce qui leur manquait sur deux sujets importants : le stylobate et la tête du mur Est.

Le stylobate (assise 7B)

L'assise plate 7A, qu'ils avaient reconstruite à l'exception de ses deux extrémités, porte des trous de pince et des cuvettes de scellement qui indiquent que l'assise superposée, 7B, était faite en façade de 23 blocs à peu près égaux. Les dalles trouvées sur place, dont certaines ont porté une colonne à peu près centrée, conviennent par leurs dimensions et leurs scellements. Donc G. Roux avait tort de les exclure et nous disons désormais « le portique

[10] Fin avril ou tout début mai 1967. Le coup d'État du 21 avril, dit « putsch des colonels », nous avait surpris à Delphes.

[11] Rien non plus sur la base des *navarques*. G. Daux avait manifesté de l'enthousiasme au début de l'été en sortant de son habituelle réserve. J'ai appris qu'il avait changé d'opinion par la suite, mais je n'ai pas vu la correspondance échangée entre lui et l'équipe.

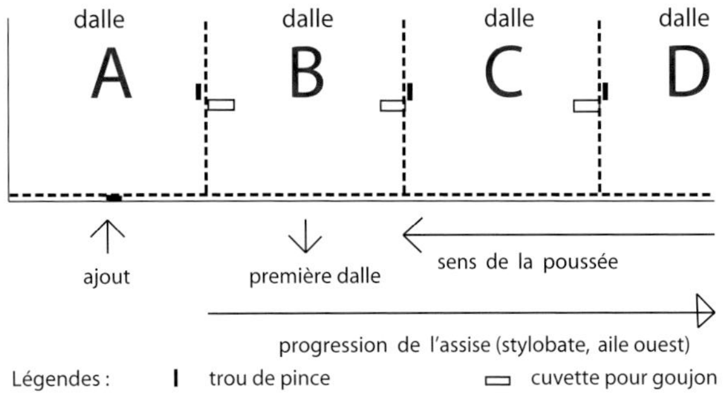

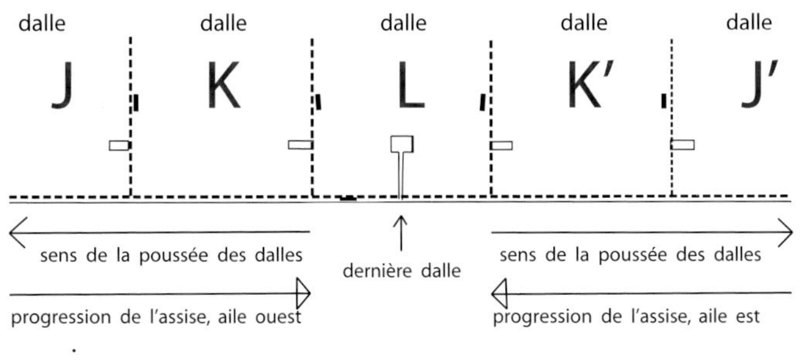

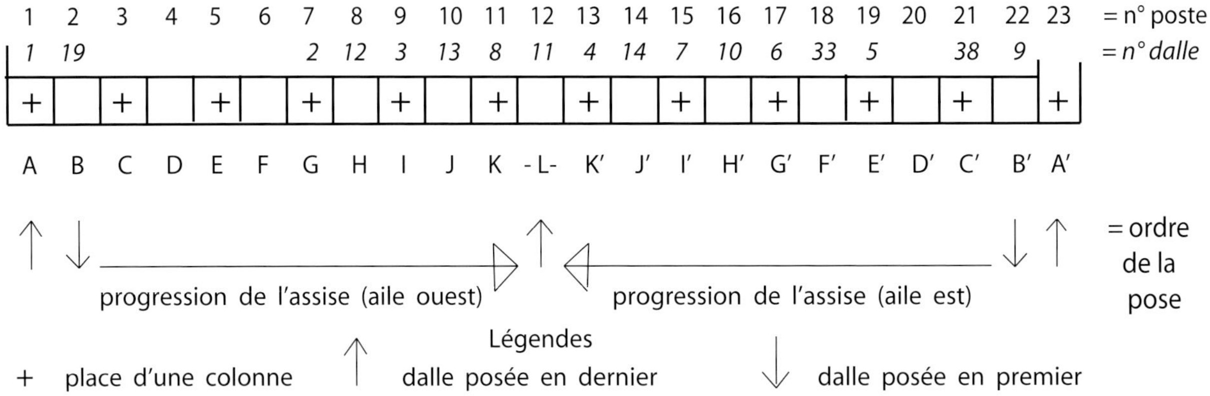

Fig. 6 (en haut à gauche). Delphes, portique 108, mise en place du stylobate 7B d'après les traces sur l'assise 7A: extrémité ouest (dessin JFB, 2009). Nord conventionnel en haut. Fig. 7 (en haut à droite). *Idem :* partie médiane (dessin JFB, 2009). Fig. 8 (en bas). *Idem* : ensemble du stylobate (dessin JFB, 2009).

108 ». Comme le recensement de tous les fragments a montré que les dalles porte-colonnes étaient au moins au nombre de 9, la restitution d'une colonnade à 8 colonnes, traditionnellement admise, devait être abandonnée pour une restitution à 12 colonnes[12]. D'après les traces conservées près de l'extrémité Ouest de l'assise 7A (Fig. 6), la mise en place a commencé en B (poste 2), où la dalle *n° 19* du dossier danois a été scellée « à joints ouverts » par deux goujons, l'un à l'Ouest et l'autre à l'Est; de ce côté, on a ajouté des dalles successivement en C, en D et ainsi de suite jusqu'en K (poste 11), en scellant chacune de ces dalles au pied de son joint Est. À l'aile Est, le dispositif était symétrique (Fig. 8) depuis C' (poste 21) jusqu'en K' (poste 13) pour les dalles avec un goujon au pied du joint Ouest cette fois; l'assise 7A est en partie perdue sous le poste 22 (B'), mais nous possédons la dalle à deux goujons *n° 9* qui correspond au *n° 19* de l'autre aile. Entre les deux ailes incomplètes BK et B'K', en L, la dalle médiane *n° 11* a été insérée par le haut[13] et scellée « à goujon perdu » depuis l'avant (Fig. 7). Les dalles des extrémités ont été ajoutées : à l'Ouest, en A, la dalle *n° 1*, qui portait une colonne à peu près sur son axe, a été placée (et peut-être scellée : cassure à gauche) entre le *n° 19* et la plate-forme d'entrée; à l'Est, en A', la dalle (perdue) étant moins large que les autres, la colonne chevauchait le joint, comme le confirme l'examen du lit d'attente du *n° 9*. Je suppose que cette dalle d'angle était plus profonde que les autres et scellée par devant et par le côté, mais l'assise 7A est ici lacunaire.

Les grandes lignes de ce schéma devaient être connues de l'équipe qui avait rétabli une partie de l'assise 7A, mais elle n'a ni remonté le stylobate 7B ni laissé le moindre croquis. Or il n'a fallu que

[12] La formule à 12 colonnes avait été proposée par H. Bulle (dessin : Pomtow, H., 1924, 1199-202). Mais celle à 8 colonnes l'avait emporté très généralement jusqu'à mon rapport à l'École Française, qui a été utilisé dès *BCH* 93 (1969), 757 fig. 9. Celle de Roux, G., 1963, fig. 34, sans colonnes, a été souvent reproduite même depuis ma reconstruction.

[13] Elle présente la particularité d'avoir des trous de pince dans les joints Est et Ouest.

Fig. 9. Delphes, portique 108, tête du mur Est : assise paire, avec le Nord à droite (cliché JFB, 1969).

Fig.10. *Idem* : assise impaire, de couronnement, avec le Nord en bas (cliché JFB, 1969).

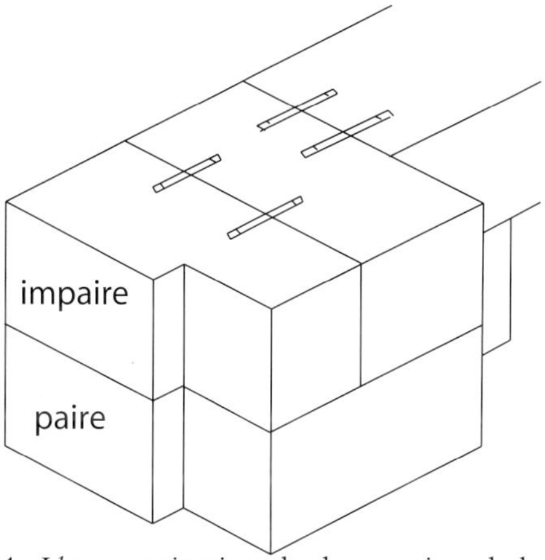

Fig. 11. *Idem* : restitution de deux assises de brèche, avec le Nord à droite (dessin JFB, 2009).

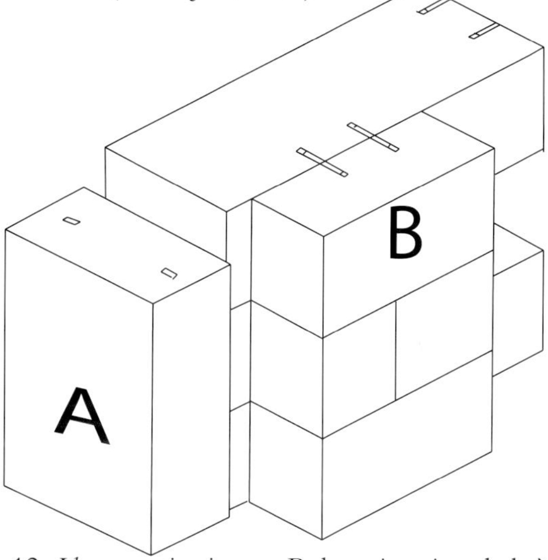

Fig. 12. *Idem* : restitution en B de trois assises de brèche et, en A, de l'ante de pôros adossée (dessin JFB, 2009).

quelques semaines à l'ignorant que j'étais pour étudier la question sans aide et pour parvenir à un projet correct de restitution du stylobate[14]. Qu'est-ce donc qui avait manqué à l'équipe ? Au *minimum*, deux détails infimes. 1° Sur l'extrémité Est de la dalle *n° 9*, les très légères traces de cannelures n'avaient pas été vues. 2° Le long fragment *n° 38* avait été interprété comme appartenant à une dalle d'une rangée intérieure à cause d'une dimension qui dépasse d'une quinzaine de centimètres le standard des dalles de la façade. L'auteur du relevé n'avait pas remarqué, dans la cassure qui a emporté la moitié du bloc, la paroi d'une cuvette pour goujon, qui incite à reconnaître une dalle porte-colonne. La situation qui en découle pour la colonne et la longueur singulière du bloc le confirment : sa place est en C' (poste 21).

La tête du mur Est

Les architectes avaient rassemblé en face du portique 16 blocs de brèche qui proviennent évidemment d'une tête de mur renforcée par un contrefort latéral (Fig. 9-12). Le lot représente dix

[14] En 1968, j'ai fait contôler ma restitution théorique par Peter Ogorelec, architecte slovène; celui-ci a fait, entre autres travaux, le relevé des tambours de colonnes (en pôros) et nous avons replacé ensemble le dallage. C'est seulement en 1970 que j'ai remis dessus un tambour de colonne avec Olivier Rollin, diplômé des Arts décoratifs de Paris.

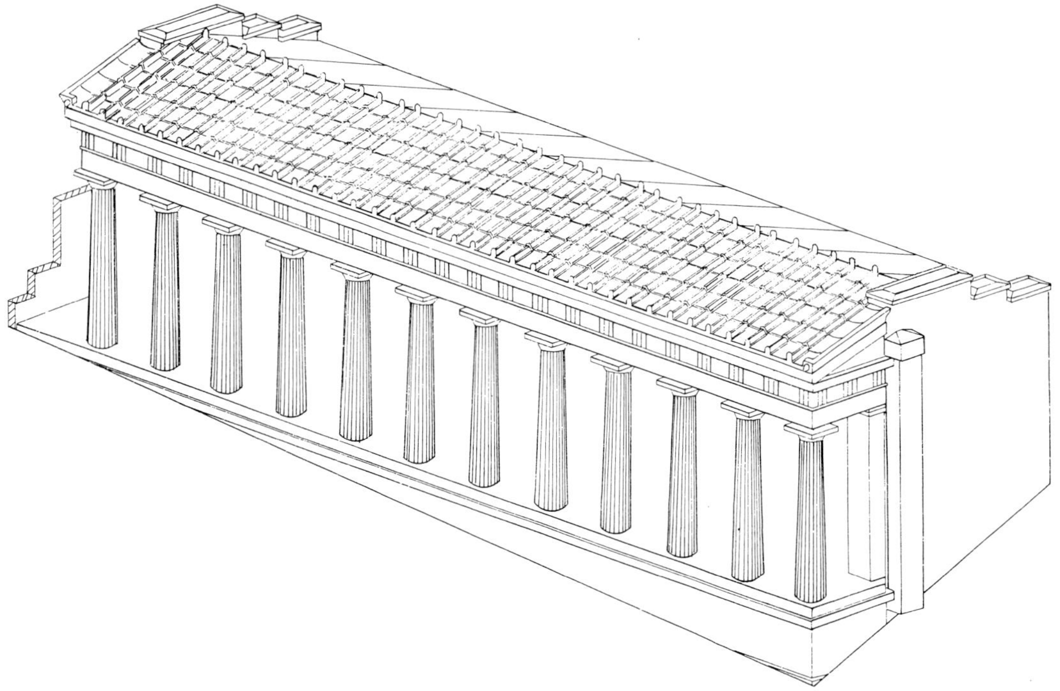

Fig. 13. Delphes, portique 108 : restitution provisoire (dessin JFB et M. Schumacher, 1993).

assises, dont celle qui comportait le couronnement du contrefort, sur lequel rien ne pouvait reposer (Fig. 10). Le plan singulier oblige à replacer ce dispositif à l'extrémité Sud du mur Est (Fig. 11), où se trouve la saillie des fondations sur laquelle s'élevait le contrefort. Cette découverte, qui leur revient, est importante de trois façons au moins : elle a un intérêt pour l'histoire de l'architecture; elle explique la saillie des fondations, jusqu'alors inexpliquée; et elle permet d'avancer dans la restitution de l'élévation, parce que ces dix assises, ou plus encore, s'élevaient au-dessus du dallage (Fig. 13). Pourtant, l'équipe n'a pas laissé le moindre document concernant ce sujet. Le nécessaire a été fait au cours de l'été 1969[15].

Plus de dix ans après, j'ai découvert qu'un grand bloc de pôros rangé dans un dépôt voisin appartenait à un pilier d'ante appuyé contre cette tête de mur (Fig. 12, bloc A). Il résulte de ce dispositif que l'ordre, en pôros, était comme plaqué devant la niche de brèche (Fig. 13). Ni ce bloc particulier ni ceux de la tête de mur n'avaient été désignés aux architectes danois. Mais les blocs de la tête du mur figuraient dans leur catalogue des blocs de brèche; au contraire, le bloc d'ante leur avait échappé d'autant plus facilement qu'ils avaient omis de dessiner les tambours de colonnes, eux aussi en pôros. C'est précisément le mode de scellement de ce bloc, comparable à celui des tambours, qui a attiré mon attention.

Concluons cette partie. E. Olsen avait certes raison de dire que *les pierres montrent d'elles-mêmes...* Le propos s'apparente à la leçon initiale de son équipe (exactitude de l'observation et exhaustivité). Celle-ci n'a pas respecté la leçon jusqu'au bout, mais est-ce anormal ? Nul n'est infaillible, même dans sa spécialité. En outre, la complexité des problèmes de l'archéologique est si patente que les chercheurs raisonnables, loin de fuir la discussion avec les spécialistes des autres disciplines, la rechercheraient plutôt.

[15] Au cours de cet été 1969, Marko Kurnik, étudiant slovène en architecture, et moi-même avons réalisé un relevé des blocs de cette tête de murs, leur groupement en assises et le classement de ces assises. Nos restitutions d'ensemble faisaient, à tort, reposer l'entablement du portique sur la tête du mur Est.

Delphes, temple d'Apollon (IVe siècle av. J.-C.)

L'étude du temple d'Apollon a suivi, depuis la fouille (années 1890), un cours plutôt cahoteux. Le projet éditorial, qui avait séparé l'architecture de la sculpture et de l'épigraphie, n'a abouti qu'en 1970. À ce moment, on savait depuis longtemps qu'il fallait reprendre deux publications déjà vieillies, celle de l'architecture du temple reconstruit au IVe siècle et celle des inscriptions relatives à cette reconstruction. Juste après, la sculpture tympanale de ce même temple a été identifiée... Si l'étude n'avait pas été fragmentée, peut-être ne serait-on parvenu à aucune publication.

Il y avait pourtant un savant qui avait tenté d'utiliser de manière systématique à la fois les sources écrites (littéraires et épigraphiques) et les données architecturales concernant ce temple : c'était G. Roux[16]. Comme ces études m'avaient paru d'un très grand intérêt, mais erronées sur plus d'un point, j'ai adressé de Strasbourg, en mai 1981, une longue lettre à J. Bousquet, qui m'a reçu chez lui, à Paris, quelques jours après. La conversation commencée alors a rebondi récemment entre E. Hansen et moi, pour trouver parfois une solution. Voici quelques exemples où l'on verra chacun entrer dans le domaine présumé de l'autre.

Les selides

L'article que cette lettre préparait visait à établir plusieurs étapes de l'histoire de la reconstruction en utilisant mieux que G. Roux les mêmes éléments[17]. En particulier, je soutenais contre lui que le péristyle du temple avait été construit avant le sèkos. Cela est maintenant confirmé par l'étude d'E. Hansen. La figure 14 reproduit une coupe sur le péristyle du temple de Tégée, avec son plafond à caissons B, en marbre comme le reste. G. Roux imaginait quelque chose de semblable au temple de Delphes, à peu près contemporain, mais fait en pôros, et croyait reconnaître les dalles de son plafond dans une série de *selides* livrées avant la guerre de 356-346 et que l'on a fini de payer après cette guerre, d'après les comptes[18]. Mais cette identification est impossible parce que le plafond devait s'appuyer sur le mur du sèkos qui n'était pas encore construit à ce moment. J'avais donc proposé à J. Bousquet de reconnaître dans les *selides* les pièces du larmier (A). Mais il m'avait opposé des raisons épigraphiques qu'il jugeait dirimantes. J'ai remarqué en 2008 seulement qu'il avait renversé ces arguments dès 1984 sans s'en apercevoir lui-même[19]. Mais, en 2004 ou 2005, E. Hansen m'a démontré trois choses au sujet de ce petit dossier : 1° le plafond du péristyle était en bois et non en pierre ; 2° la contre-frise était constituée par quatre assises de blocs ordinaires et non par de grandes dalles dressées sur chant ; 3° ces deux faits et la progression du chantier telle qu'on la connaît imposent de voir dans les *selides* les pièces du larmier.

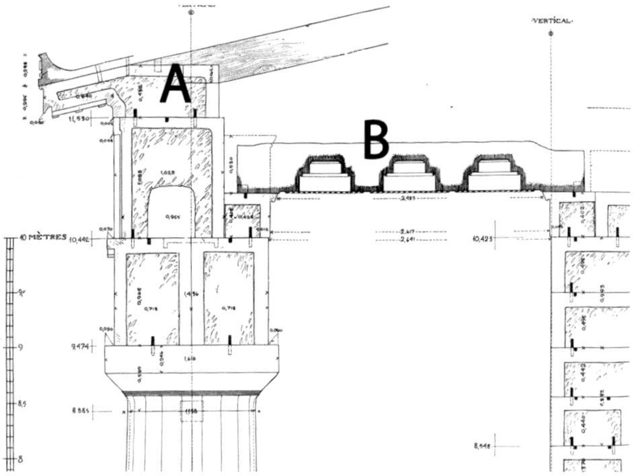

Fig. 14. Tégée, temple, extrait d'une coupe restituée sur le péristyle : A, larmier; B, plafond à caissons; en marbre l'un et l'autre (M. Clemmensen, dessin 1913-1914, publ. 1924, © EFA).

Conclusions partielles. 1° Ici, c'est l'architecte qui enseigne aux philologues le sens des mots. 2° Connaissant le prix de ces pièces, je peux désormais communiquer à l'architecte celui d'autres blocs

[16] Roux, G., 1966 et 1979. Au contraire, P. Amandry, dont les travaux sur le temple font autorité depuis 1941, s'est montré réservé au sujet de l'utilisation des textes : voir notamment Amandry, P. ,1992 & 1997.

[17] Bommelaer, J.-Fr., 1983.

[18] Roux, G., 1979, 206. Voir *CID*, **34 I**, 42 & 47; **57**, 15.

[19] Voir Bousquet, J., 1984, 138 et 140.

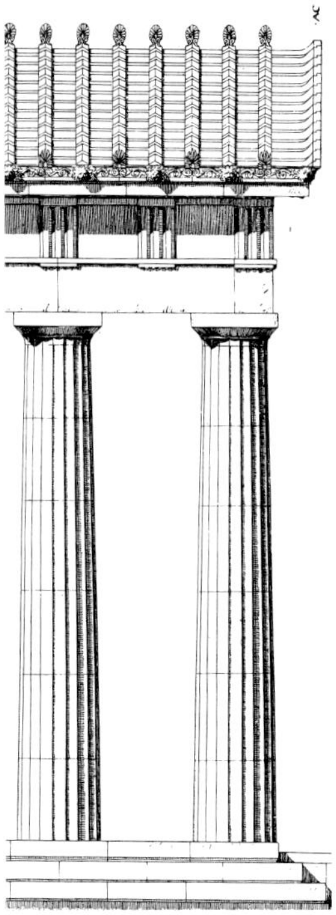

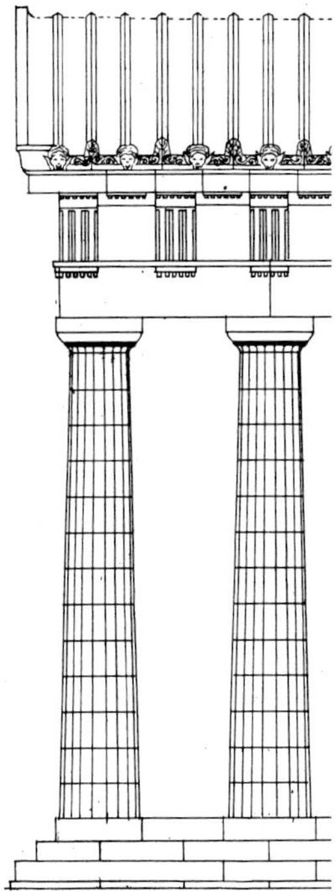

Fig. 15. Restitution de l'ordre extérieur et de la couverture de deux temples du IVe siècle :
a : Tégée, avec gargouille à l'angle (dessin M. Clemmensen, publ. 1924, © EFA);
b : Delphes, avec gargouille décalée (dessin H. Lacoste, publ. 1920, © EFA).

de l'entablement originel et le surcoût des blocs angulaires de larmier « plus gros » commandés en remplacement quelques années plus tard[20].

Les triglyphes angulaires du sékos

Les comptes nous apprennent qu'on a commandé de nouveaux « triglyphes » angulaires pour le sèkos, eux aussi plus chers parce qu'ils étaient plus gros que ceux de la commande initiale[21]. Les modernes avaient tendance à restituer des blocs de plan carré, avec un triglyphe sur la façade et un sur le retour, sans métope attachée. Mais il apparaît désormais que les nouveaux venus étaient plus chers que les pièces de l'entablement extérieur, quoique moins hauts. C'est pourquoi j'ai demandé à E. Hansen de leur restituer, comme G. Roux[22], une contre-métope (passant derrière la métope) et probablement une queue pour les lier au mur.

J'ajoute que, dans tout ce dossier des blocs commandés à nouveau, la mise en place des nouveaux triglyphes est la seule opération au sujet de laquelle on ne qualifie pas le paiement de « renouvelé ». J'y vois le signe que les blocs de la première série n'avaient pas été mis en place : c'est probablement à leur arrivée à Delphes, lors de l'été ou de l'automne de 338, que l'architecte a changé le projet de son prédécesseur.

La syggrophos

Le mot *syggrophos* se trouve une vingtaine de fois dans le *corpus*, toujours précédé d'une préposition signifiant *conformément à* ou *contrairement à*. J. Bousquet l'a traduit généralement par *contrat*. Mais E. Hansen m'a dit plusieurs fois à peu près ce qui suit : « ce dont on avait surtout besoin au moment de l'adjudication des travaux, c'était d'un *projet* d'architecte décrivant ce qu'il y avait à faire, accepté par les autorités, et ainsi transformé en *cahier des charges* ». J'ai revu tous les passages. De fait, les cas où il faut traduire le mot par *contrat* sont rares et le dossier des blocs refaits plus gros devient clair avec *cahier des charges.* Dans ce dossier, tous les travaux ont été faits deux fois et (à l'exception de la pose des triglyphes angulaires) payés deux fois. La différence entre les deux phases est que les contrats de la première étaient conformes au cahier des charges, alors que ceux de la deuxième ont été établis *en dérogation au cahier des charges* parce qu'on voulait des blocs *plus gros* : les prix ont été majorés en fonction de l'augmentation des dimensions. Enfin, on ne sait pas si le cahier des charges comportait la définition des prix : je ne le crois pas, mais le point reste douteux alors que tout le reste est éclairé par la traduction d'E. Hansen.

Les têtes de lions

Un autre compte appelle *têtes de lions* le chéneau horizontal avec ses gargouilles, lesquelles ont

---

[20] On verra Bommelaer, J.-Fr., 2009, pour les références et pour le raisonnement.
[21] Voir *CID*, **59 I**, 41-50 et& 60-9; **II**, 3-16; **62 II B** 65-73.
[22] Roux, G., 1966, 292. Bien entendu, l'auteur ne connaissait pas les prix récemment établis.

cette forme, selon la coutume[23]. Il nous apprend que l'Athénien Molossos a reçu son deuxième et dernier paiement pour les *têtes de lions* en 341. Cela signifie que le chéneau était alors livré en entier. Il a sûrement été monté aussitôt[24].

Il nous en reste de nombreux fragments, en marbre. L'un d'eux permet de connaître la longueur totale d'une pièce, soit 1,53 m. Cette longueur paraît avoir été modulaire, parce qu'elle représente les trois quarts du couple Métope + Triglyphe ou les trois huitièmes d'un entraxe de la colonnade. Cela a amené H. Lacoste à la restitution présentée à la figure 15. Cependant, je me suis aperçu que J. Bousquet s'était posé avant moi le petit problème que voici[25]. H. Lacoste avait restitué 78 gargouilles en tout, donc 39 par long côté du temple. Mais le prix total indiqué par le compte est de 8.400 drachmes. Certes, il pourrait s'agir d'un prix «rond» de 120 Mines ou 2 Talents. Mais on attendrait plutôt, d'après l'usage, un prix «à la pièce». Or le nombre 8.400 ne se divise pas par 78. En revanche, la division par 80 donnerait un prix de 105 drachmes (1½ Mine) par pièce. Ayant écrit cela, J. Bousquet s'est tout de même rallié à la solution Lacoste 3 x 2, sans doute par révérence à l'égard de l'architecte.

Cette solution Lacoste est contestable pour une raison architecturale. Le retour de la moulure du chéneau rampant sur une bonne longueur jusqu'à la première (ou dernière) gargouille du long côté, serait acceptable si ce long côté était dépourvu de chéneau horizontal entre ses deux extrémités. Mais ici, le chéneau horizontal existe, avec un profil et un décor différents de celui du rampant : la formule architecturale appropriée me paraît être celle qui est attestée au temple d'Aléa à Tégée, avec une gargouille à chacun des quatre angles inférieurs du toit, donc réservant une forme de chéneau à la façade et l'autre au long côté (Fig. 15a). En appliquant cette formule à Delphes, on passerait de 39 x 2 *têtes de lions* à 40 x 2. Que les pièces extrêmes aient eu une longueur particulière importe peu : tel était le cas à Tégée, où M. Clemmensen en avait trouvé un exemplaire.

Conclusion

Les leçons de 1967 ont été non seulement confirmées, mais encore complétées par celle-ci : la discussion est une nécessité. Combien de fois l'architecte a sollicité le littéraire et historien que je suis, et accepté de bon cœur mes critiques, même en matière d'architecture ! Combien de fois en revanche c'est lui qui a eu raison, non seulement au sujet de l'agencement des pierres, mais même sur le sens des mots antiques ! J'ai été heureux d'avoir l'occasion de vous en montrer quelques cas, qui me paraissent exemplaires d'une collaboration utile et en même temps agréable, dans laquelle la spécialité de chacun a moins compté que la volonté commune de découvrir la vérité[26].

---

[23] Compte *CID*, **32**, 10-1; image du chéneau : Lacoste, H., 1920, pl. IX.

[24] On notera que cela a été fait avant l'achèvement du mur du sèkos.

[25] Bousquet, J., 1988, 55.

[26] Addendum. La solution Lacoste a été adoptée par Hansen, E., 2010, fig.18.18.

Note complémentaire

À propos de la tholos de Delphes

Le toit

Il y a deux séries de blocs de chéneaux assez semblables, mais de dimensions différentes.

K. Gottlob avait bien observé qu'une des deux séries était beaucoup moins usée que l'autre. Il avait tiré de cette observation une conclusion raisonnable : un premier toit avait duré peu de temps, avant d'être remplacé par un second toit qui a duré beaucoup plus longtemps (*FD* II, 1925, sous la plume de J. Charbonneaux).

F. Kirk a travaillé avec G. Roux. Celui-ci a cru pouvoir publier dans le *BCH* de 1952 que les deux chéneaux ont appartenu à un même toit, comme l'avait écrit H. Pomtow en son temps, mais avec un autre dispositif. Sauf erreur de ma part, G. Roux donnait une restitution en coupe, mais non en élévation. Cet article avait le mérite d'identifier des socles d'acrotères.

K. Gottlob a dessiné en 1962 un brouillon d'élévation et une perspective aquarellée, mises au goût du jour (colonnes doriques plus hautes, toit à deux chéneaux, mais sans les acrotères basses) qui ont dormi dans des cartons. L'aquarelle en est ressortie à l'époque du centenaire des fouilles de Delphes, dans *Archéologia*, et l'élévation dans le catalogue de l'exposition.

La première élévation publiée avec les colonnes hautes et les deux chéneaux doit être celle que D. Laroche a donnée en 1990 pour le *Guide de Delphes, le Site* (*SD*) que j'ai fait paraître courant 1991. Bien que nous ayons beaucoup travaillé ensemble sur ce monument, nous ignorions encore que F. Kirk n'avait pas été d'accord avec G. Roux, à cause de l'état différent des deux séries de blocs.

Mais, dès l'été de 1991, D. Laroche a revu les blocs et fait le même constat que ses deux prédécesseurs danois. Au colloque strasbourgeois du centenaire de la fouille (novembre 1991), il nous a fait connaître l'article de F. Kirk, «Marmortag paa Tholos in Delphi», *Tilegnet Mogens Koch* (1968), p. 211 ss., en développant son argumentation et son illustration pour conclure de la même manière : deux toits successifs, le premier, à huit pans très distincts («couverture octogonale»), était entouré par le «petit» chéneau à bords découpés ; le second, à tuiles «radiales», donc d'aspect plus cônique, était entouré par le «grand» chéneau à bord rectiligne : voir D. Laroche in *Delphes centenaire*... éd. J.-Fr. Bommelaer, *Travaux du CRPOGA* 12 (1992), p. 207-221.

Depuis lors nous avons continué de travailler à cette question, parmi d'autres. Chacun des deux schémas suppose une pente du toit constante. Mais il reste une tuile qui ne s'intègre ni dans l'un ni dans l'autre. Nous pensons à une forme «en trompette», qui est attestée ailleurs : on se reportera á la prochaine édition du *Guide*.

Colonnes

Extérieures. J'ai évoqué au passage les colonnes doriques «plus hautes» que K. Gottlob ne l'avait cru (comme déjà l'architecte de H. Pomtow, que cet architecte ait été H. Bulle ou un autre). Nous sommes bien certains qu'elles étaient au nombre de 20 et disposées avec la plus grande régularité. Leur anastylose avec 5 tambours et non plus 4 (1938) est parfois mise en doute. C'est pourquoi j'ai obtenu d'EDF qu'on scanne une de ces colonnes sur toute sa hauteur en 1996 : s'il y avait eu le moindre à-coup dans le tracé d'une cannelure, cela serait apparu. Voir *Guide de Marmaria* (1997), où cependant je ne garantis que ce que j'ai écrit moi-même.

Intérieures. On est stupéfié de lire sous la plume de J. Charbonneaux que les colonnes intérieures doivent avoir été au nombre de 10 pour la seule raison qu'il y avait 20 colonnes extérieures, alors que cela a obligé la dessinateur de *FD* à découper le cercle intérieur en 11 parties (à cause de la largeur de la porte, qui équivaut dans ce cas à deux entraxes, montants compris), donc sans rapport avec la position des colonnes extérieures. On a l'impression que, ici aussi, K. Gottlob a eu la main forcée.

Pour des raisons architecturales (densité des colonnes et support de la charpente), j'estime que le découpage du cercle intérieur était en 16 parties : d'où, au premier niveau, 13 colonnes + 2 montants de porte + un support absent dans l'axe de la porte. De surcroît, nous superposons aux colonnes corinthiennes connues une petite colonnade d'étage. Voir *Guide de Marmaria* avec la même réserve que ci-avant.

À propos du théâtre

De T. Gunnarson, j'ai lu le résumé qui avait été diffusé et ce qui est imprimé dans le catalogue qu'E. Hansen m'a envoyé. Heureusement, on peut toujours recourir aux planches 17, 19 et 20 de *FD II, Atlas*, planches excellentes dont il a dessiné la plus grande partie (ne pas oublier 19).

La première rangée de gradins de ce théâtre repose sur un podium haut de 1,02 m au lieu d'être au ras de l'orchestra, comme c'est le cas normal dans les théâtres grecs. La première réaction est de se demander s'il s'agirait d'une transformation d'époque romaine. C'est cette réaction que T. Gunnarson présente comme une hypothèse raisonnable, sinon comme une certitude (voir ci-après p. 71 et Fig. 3). Plusieurs raisons s'y opposent.

1° La première est d'ordre très général : lorsque l'époque romaine a fait de telles transformations, c'était pour mettre les spectateurs à l'abri de spectacles dangereux. Par conséquent, on créait un dénivelé beaucoup plus important. J'en ai vu récemment un exemple en Libye, à Cyrène si je ne m'abuse, et plus anciennement à Xanthos : rien à voir.*

2° L'arc de cercle que décrit le front du dispositif actuel (une marche d'ecalier dépassant en avant du podium) atteint à ses extrémités le point exact qui convient, c'est-à-dire l'extrémité des murs des *parodoi*, juste derrière la base de statue, qui est libre. Si, par hypothèse, il y avait eu deux gradins de plus, ils auraient abouti contre ces bases d'une façon bizarre et qui aurait laissé des traces. Ces bases sont bien à leur place et porteuses d'inscriptions qui commencent au IIe siècle av. J.-C.

3° Le podium, les 4 marches qui lui correspondent dans les 8 escaliers et le caniveau ont été construits en calcaire de Saint Élie, contrairement au reste du théâtre. Cet ensemble de plusieurs centaines de blocs provient du bâtiment n° 609, qui est situé juste à l'Est du théâtre, ou pour mieux dire, à l'Est et sous le mur Est du théâtre. Certaines cuvettes de scellement en position inutile attestent cette provenance. Ce bâtiment 609 a été construit dans la deusième moitié du IVe siècle, comme le prouvent sa technique et la signature d'un entrepreneur connu au temple d'Apollon. Il a été détruit probablement par une avalanche de rochers; en tout cas, plusieurs gros rochers s'appuient sur ses restes. La construction du théâtre a été commencée après cette destruction. Elle a commencé par les murs de soutènement dont on avait besoin en premier, c'est-à-dire la partie basse des murs des *parodoi* et le mur Est, dont le tracé passe sur le côté Ouest de 609.

Le podium est composé de deux assises plates de 26 cm encadrant une assise haute (orthostate de 52 cm). Cette assise, qui est complète, était entièrement posée et en cours de scellement quand un accident est survenu. Bien que tous les crampons aient été arrachés ultérieurement, nous pouvons raisonner sur les cuvettes, toutes visibles (certaines se voient sur l'excellent relevé de *FD* II, *Atlas*). Quelques cuvettes n'étaient pas encore creusées (tel bloc a sa cuvette de crampon à un bout et non à l'autre), mais la plupart l'étaient. Il arrive aussi qu'on trouve les deux moitiés d'une cuvette pour crampon qui sont en discordance : ainsi au Nord de la *kerkis* située le plus à l'Est; ou encore une demi-cuvette à laquelle rien ne correspond : ainsi au Sud de la 2ème *kerkis* Ouest. Ces deux exemples sont visibles sur l'*Atlas*; j'en ai donné ailleurs un relevé complet. Ils nous apprennent que le travail était inachevé quand un séisme ou quelque chose du même genre a renversé une partie de l'assise et que, ultérieurement on a réinséré les blocs sortis de place, en travaillant assez mal, y compris en remettant certains d'entre eux à l'envers et sans finir le scellement commencé.

Le relevé nous a appris autre chose : la partie Nord du mur Est, qui grimpait droit vers le Nord, a été abandonnée : on a resserré le plan de la partie haute du théâtre. Aujourd'hui, ce tronçon de mur est enterré. À l'angle Sud-Ouest aussi, on voit un changement d'orientation qui correspond à un resserrement du plan.

Quand cela est-il arrivé ? Après la construction (achevée ou non) de 609 et sa destruction. Avant les premières inscriptions du théâtre, qui datent de la deusième moitié du IIe siècle av. J.-C. Et même avant la première des lettres envoyée par les Delphiens au roi de Pergame (dossier de 159-158 : appel à l'aide; réponse avec promesses ; honneurs décrétés en retour). Il y est question de la «construction» ou de la «réparation» du théâtre et des monuments voisins. C'est l'argent des rois de Pergame qui a permis de terminer la construction à partir de cette date. Comme ils ont envoyé des esclaves (qu'il fallait nourrir) et que le travail paraît bâclé, cela n'a pas dû durer très longtemps.

G. Roux pensait que le théâtre datait du IVe siècle à cause des crampons en forme de double T, dont nous savons maintenant qu'ils imitaient ceux du bâtiment 609.

* On entend souvent les guides professionnels expliquer aux touristes de Delphes qu'il y avait là des naumachies; mais on ne les entend jamais expliquer comment l'eau était retenue, alors que les *parodoi* sont ouvertes...

Bibliographie

Amandry, P., 1992
« Où était l'omphalos ? », dans *Delphes, centenaire de la « Grande Fouille » réalisée par l'École Française d'Athènes (1892-1903),* colloque Strasbourg 1991, Actes du CRPOGA 12, J.-Fr. Bommelaer (éd.), 177-205 = P. Amandry et E. Hansen, *Le temple d'Apollon du IVe siècle* (*Fouilles de Delphes* II), 2010, 85-100.

Amandry, P., 1997
« Recherches sur la cella du temple de Delphes », dans *Oracles et prophéties dans l'Antiquité,* colloque Strasbourg 1995, Actes du CRPOGA 15, J.G. Heintz (éd.), 271-82 = P. Amandry et E. Hansen, *Le temple d'Apollon du IVe siècle* (*Fouilles de Delphes* II), 2010, 73-86.

Bommelaer, J.-Fr., 1971
« Note sur les «Navarques» et les successeurs de Polyclète à Delphes », *BCH* 95, 43-64.

Bommelaer, J.-Fr., 1981
Lysandre de Sparte, histoire et traditions (BEFAR 240), Paris.

Bommelaer, J.-Fr., 1983
« La construction du temple classique de Delphes », *BCH* 107, 191-206.

Bommelaer, J.-Fr., 2009
« Delphica 1 », *BCH* à paraître

Bousquet, J., 1984
« Les comptables de Delphes et le dixième de garantie », in *Hommages à Lucien Lerat,* Centre de recherches d'histoire ancienne, 55, Besançon, 135-43.

Bousquet, J., 1988
Études sur les comptes de Delphes (BEFAR 267), Paris.

Bousquet, J., 1989
Les comptes du quatrième et du troisième siècle (*Corpus des inscriptions de Delphes,* II), Paris.

Dugas, E., J. Berchmans & M. Clemmensen, 1924
Le sanctuaire d'Aléa Athéna à Tégée au IVe siècle, Paris.

Hallager, E. & D. Mulliez (eds.) 2008
Une liaison française – 100 années de présence d' architects danois à l' École française d'Athènes, Athens.

Hansen, E., G. Algreen-Ussing & *alii*, 1975
Topographie et architecture, Sanctuaire d'Apollon, Atlas (*Fouilles de Delphes,* II), Paris.

Lacoste, H., 1920
La terrasse du temple, 1, relevés et restaurations (*Fouilles de Delphes,* II), Paris.

Pomtow, H., 1924
« Delphoi: Die Topographie (erste Hälfte) », dans *RE Suppl. 4,* 1189-1432.

Roux, G., 1961
L'architecture de l'Argolide aux IVe et IIIe siècles avant J.-C. (BEFAR 199), Paris.

Roux, G., 1963
« Les Navarques » dans *Énigmes à Delphes,* J. Pouilloux & G. Roux, Paris, 16-36.

Roux, G., 1966
« Les comptes du IVe siècle et la reconstruction du temple d'Apollon à Delphes », *RA* 1966, 245-96.

Roux, G., 1979
L'amphictionie, Delphes et le temple d'Apollon au IVe siècle (Collection de la Maison de l'Orient méditerranéen, 8), Lyon.

Roux, G., 1989
'Problèmes delphiques d'architecture et d'épigraphie : I. les 'selides' du temple d'Apollon', *RA* 1989, 23-43.

The theatre at Delphi and the Reykjavík City Theatre

Þorsteinn Gunnarsson

The concept of the Greek theatre applies to more than one type of theatre. For convenience these types are often grouped into three main categories: firstly, the theatre of the Athenian Golden Age, characteristic of Greek theatrical culture in the fifth century BC; secondly, the Hellenistic theatre, which came into existence during the period 323-146 BC, when a number of places outside Greece proper took over the leadership role in Greek culture; and finally the "Graeco-Roman" theatre, which developed from the mid-second century BC, after Greece came under Roman influence and Greek culture went into a decline.

Fig. 1. The Theatre at Delfi and the Phedriades cliffs.

No two Greek theatres are the same: topography varies from site to site and the theatres themselves are of different sizes, types and dates; in addition, the components of the structures are combined in a multitude of ways in each case. Yet they are variations on a theme: a form of theatre which has sometimes been termed a democratic theatre for the masses.

The theatre at Delphi is believed to have been built around 160 BC, during the Hellenistic period.[1] In its complete form it seated about 3,700 people – a relatively small theatre for the time. In the early 1900s the theatre was surveyed and plans drawn to a scale of 1:100. My own survey plans, on which my discussion is based, were made in 1963-64 to a scale of 1:50, under the supervision of the architect Erik Hansen.[2]

The theatre stands high up in the sanctuary, at the northwest, enclosed on two sides by the walls of the sanctuary. It commands splendid panoramic views, to the nearby ruins of the temple and beyond them a deep valley of olive trees, and then down to the distant lowlands and the sea.

Ancient Greek architects have long been admired for their ability to adapt their buildings to the landscape, combining the manmade with the natural to create an artistic whole. Examples abound of this Greek expertise, but the finest

[1] Robertson 1959, 335.

[2] Hansen, Algreen-Ussing *et al.* 1975, plan 20 & coupe 5c; Gunnarsson 1991, 219-239.

Fig. 2. The orchestra. Paving and balustrade.

example is undoubtedly the Acropolis in Athens and its buildings. With respect to theatre structures, there can be few buildings which conform so well to the natural features as the theatre Delphi. The surroundings resemble a gigantic amphitheatre. The sanctuary is about 600 m above sea level and above it, on three sides, rise the Phedriades cliffs and Mount Parnassos. From a distance the rows of seats appear to be cut from the rock; so skilfully is the theatre incorporated into the landscape of the mountain that visually it does not end until the mountaintop meets the sky (Fig. 1).

When this theatre was built, the Greeks had accumulated extensive experience in theatre-building and indeed the structure bears witness to the skill of its creator. The builder was completely familiar with the requirements of the time for the function of the building and, in addition, he had a fine sense of form and space. Various details of the structure provide evidence of skilled technique. The entire theatre is constructed of limestone, the most abundant form of rock in the region. The blocks of stone are hewn with a pick chisel, then dressed as necessary using a tooth chisel and flat chisel.

Like other ancient Greek theatres, the Delphi theatre comprises three components: the *orchestra* (dance stage), the *theatron* (audience seating area) and the *skene* (stage). There is no indication that the Greeks ever set out to combine the three components into a single structure – as the Romans did in due course. They appear, on the contrary, to have sought to link them together loosely, complying with the laws of architecture.

The *orchestra* at Delphi is horseshoe-shaped and fully paved. The paving is irregular, but the paving stones have been chosen with care and fitted closely together. The floor is highest in the centre, domed, with a slight slope for drainage. The floor is surrounded by a stone balustrade, around 80 cm in height and 20 cm thick, which slots into a groove in the floor (Fig. 2). The balustrade, which collapsed long ago, was partially reconstructed at the beginning of the last century. The balustrade was undoubtedly added by the Romans, who adapted Greek theatres to their own purposes, using the *orchestra* as a setting for gladiatorial combat and fights with wild animals. The barrier was erected to protect the spectators.[3] On the outside of the balustrade is an open drain extending around a little more than a semicircle and connecting to a closed drain on the western side. Outside the drain is a pavement, one step up from the floor of the *orchestra*.

Around the pavement is a one-metre-high plinth beneath the first row of seats; this is unlike the ar-

[3] Dyggve 1949, 27.

rangement of the typical Greek theatre, where the front row is generally on a level with the *orchestra*. This disposition entails that the lowest steps are shallower, with a higher rise, than is the rule elsewhere in the theatre. Thus it is entirely reasonable to ask whether all is as it should be.

According to sources, in the period 211-217 AD, the Romans removed the lowest rows of seats in the theatre of Corinth, making it into an amphitheatre of sorts. The same is true of the theatres in Assos, Magnesia, Pergamon, and elsewhere.[4] If the Delphi theatre was altered in this manner by the Romans, three rows of seats were probably removed; and the height of three rows would in fact be equivalent to the height of the present plinth (Fig. 3). No firm conclusion can be drawn on this issue without further research.

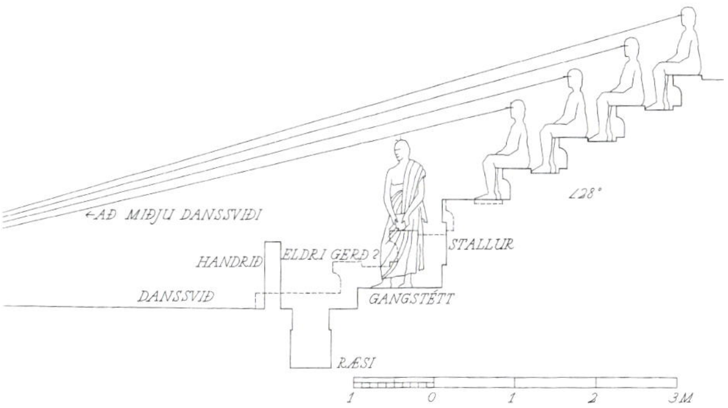

Fig. 3. Cross section showing the lowest part of the theatron.

I incline to the view, however, that the theatre was originally built in this form. I have three main reasons for this view: firstly, the front rows of seats show a higher quality of construction than the others in the theatre; secondly, the position of the *skene* is consistent with the rules on the distance from the front row of seating to the edge of the *skene* (I will return to this point in due course); and thirdly, the plinth beneath the front row displays the same technique as the plinth beneath the upper tier of the theatre, which serves to make it possible for spectators in the bottom rows to see the action, in spite of the *diazoma* or aisle in front of them. The lower plinth may well have served precisely the same purpose, that is, to enable latecomers to reach their seats without disturbing those who were already seated.

The *theatron* (audience seating area) in Delphi is mostly well preserved, although on both sides the outermost ends of many seating rows have subsided and are lost (Fig. 4). All the seating rows are concentric, departing from the rules expounded

[4] Bieber 1961, 216.

Fig. 4. The theatron.

Fig. 5. Vitruvius´s rule of theatre design.

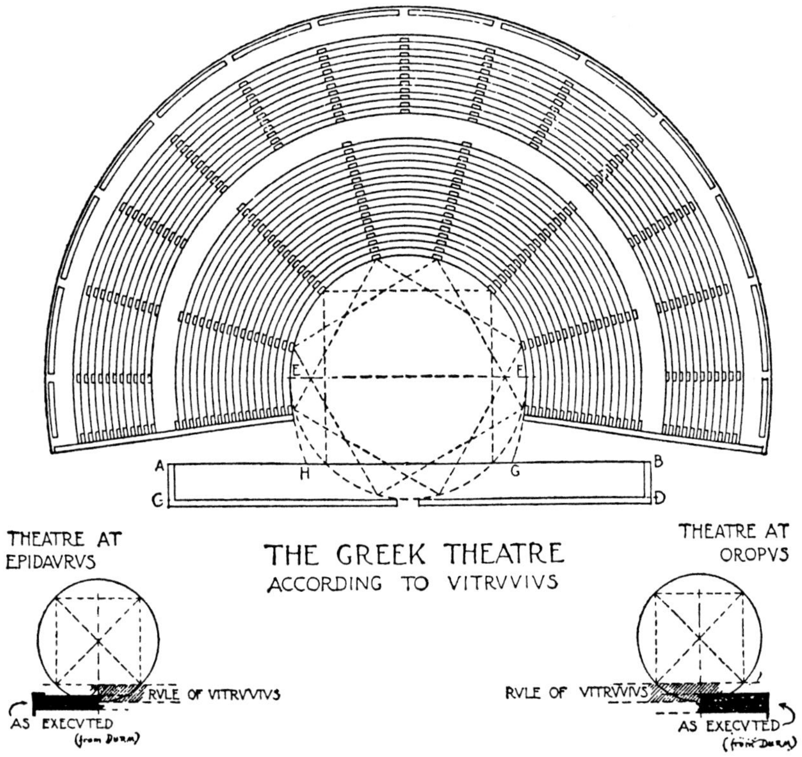

by Vitruvius for the Greek theatre. According to Vitruvius the arc of the *theatron* should be extended beyond the semicircle, using a new focus with double the original radius[5] (Fig. 5). The *theatron* comprises seven sectors of 30°. The front row of seating surrounds seven-twelfths of the *orchestra* , an arc of 210°. At the south side the *theatron* is truncated by two symmetrical supporting walls (*analemmata*), the top of which follows the slope of the seating. The *analemmata* are not, however, placed like the steps, radiating from the centre; if extrapolated, they would meet at an obtuse angle about three metres south of the centre of the theatre (Fig. 6).

Spectators entered the theatre via two passages or *parodoi* between the *analemmata* and the *orchestra*. These led to the pavement and thence to the stairs between the seats. At Delphi a grand stairway leads to the theatre, and this seems to have been the original access route. Another entrance point was placed high up, via a gate in the wall of the sanctuary, leading to the curved *diazoma*, 1.80 m across, which divides the upper from the lower tier. The upper tier is designed as an annular sector, whose area is equivalent to that of three sectors of the lower tier. On the upper tier, flights of steps lead up through the rows of seats – each flight of steps in the lower tier continues in the upper tier, and between them are additional flights of steps dividing each section of the annular sector, in accord with the rules described by Vitruvius. The rows of seats are truncated at both ends: by the wall of the sanctuary at one end, and by another wall at the other. The upper tier comprises eight rows of seats, the lower 27 (Fig. 7). For comparison, the theatre at Epidavros, generally regarded as the finest ancient Greek theatre,[6] has 34 rows in the lower tier and 21 in the upper, which is almost equivalent to the golden section.[7] With regard to these factors, we must remember the very different topography of the two sites. At Delphi, the cliffs were a crucial factor, while at Epidavros, the architect Polyclitos the Younger had nothing above him but the sky and no walls to prevent him from extending the theatre at will, in keeping with the laws of art and geometry.

In Delphi, the *theatron* displays many interesting features, of which a few will be mentioned here. The seats are cut with great accuracy. The rows of

5 Vitruvius *De Architectura* V.7.

6 Lawrence 1962, 283-284.

7 Izenour 1977, 173-175; Kirk 1955.

Fig. 6. Plan of Delfi Theatre. Survey and plans by the author.

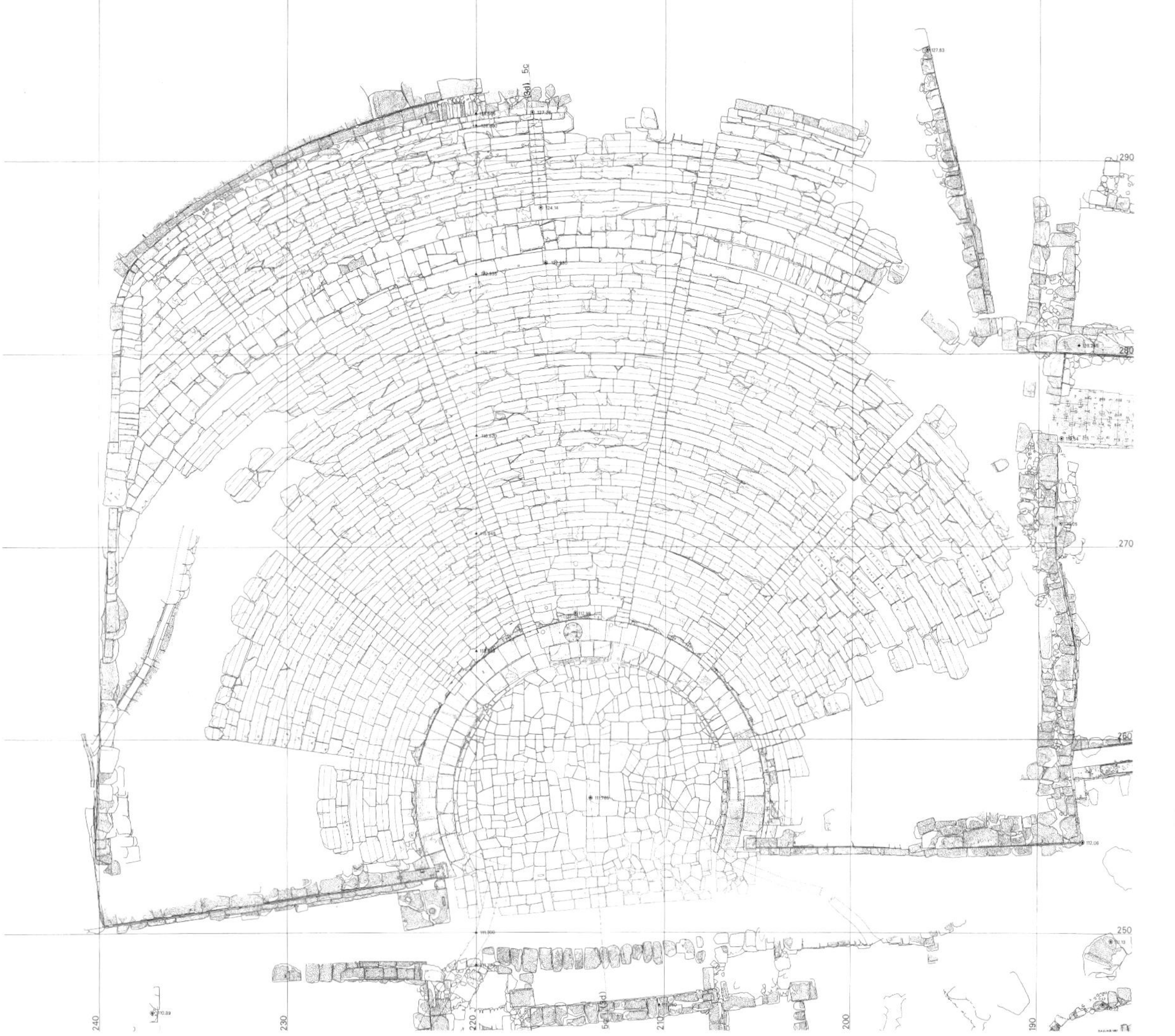

Fig. 7. Cross section of Delfi Theatre. Survey and plans by the author.

seats are spaced 68.5 cm apart; the front part is the actual seat, behind which is a pathway, set lower. Behind the pathway is a strip 10 cm wide, the same height as the seat, above which is the projecting front of the next row of seats. The seats are 37 cm high, and the lower section of the *theatron* slopes at an angle of 28°. As in other theatres, the upper tier is more steeply-pitched than the lower. This improves visibility from the upper rows and also adds to the visual impact of the structure. At Delphi, the upper slope is 32°. This is achieved not by raising the seats as at Epidavros, but by reducing the space between the rows, so that spectators in the upper tiers must have had little leg-room and had to sit with their feet tucked back under the seat (Fig 8).

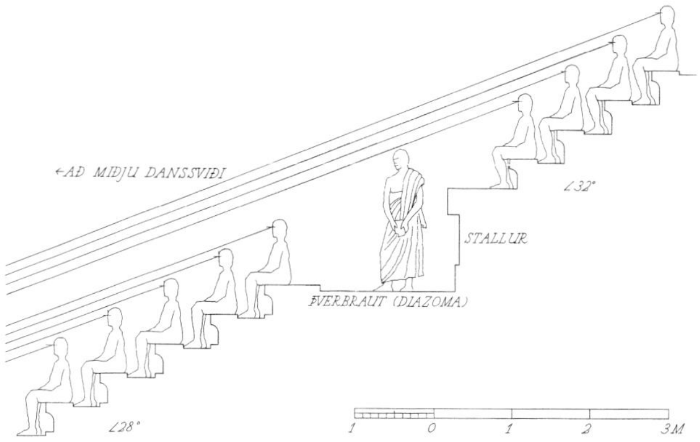

Fig. 8. Cross section showing *diazoma* with lower and upper tiers.

Another factor which is not immediately noticeable, but is of technical importance, is drainage. Firstly, the seats slope slightly backwards and the pathway behind is cut so that it is at its most shallow at the centre of the row and deepest at the steps at either end. When it rains in Delphi, it is fascinating to see how the rainwater is ingeniously drained off along the seats and pathways, down the steps and finally into the drain around the *orchestra*.

In Greek theatres, it was customary to build the front rows of seats with especial care, as this was where officials sat. At Delphi the higher status of the front seats is signalled in the subtlest manner, by tapering the projecting front of the seats at each end. In early times, there was also a ceremonial box in the middle of the theatre for the patron of the play. When the theatre was excavated around 1900, the box had disappeared; the gap has now been filled with seats from elsewhere in the *theatron*.

By 1963, many of the inscriptions which had been found on the seats of the theatre when it was studied in the early 1900s[8] appeared to have been effaced since the theatre was opened to the public.

[8] Homolle *et al*. 1902 and continuing.

Fig. 9. The orchestra and foundation of skene.

Fig. 10. The Theatre of Oropos. Columns supporting the floor of *proskenion*.

But by using side-lighting at night it proved possible to confirm that all the known inscriptions were still present; previously unknown inscriptions were also found, on the top or front of the seats. In some cases the same inscription was repeated on several consecutive seats in a row: for instance the word ΑΡΧΗΙΔΟΣ, cut into rows 4 to 10 in the second-outermost sector in the west, the area allocated to the temple priestesses of Delphi. In one place a spectator has scratched a gaming board into the stone, indicating that "the play's the thing" may not have been true for everybody in the audience.

At several points in the upper rows, holes have been made in the front of seats for guy ropes; this was done in Roman times, when awnings were often erected over theatres.

Like so many other buildings in the sanctuary, the *skene* (stage building) of the Delphi theatre has vanished, leaving only the foundation (Fig. 9). Its exterior dimensions were about 9x20 m, and the front of the *skene* was nearly 8 m from the centre of the *orchestra*. This is consistent with Vitruvius's rule on the location of the *skene*: the front of the *skene* should touch a circle drawn through the front edge of the first row of seats, and the front of the *proskenion* (front stage) should touch a square drawn within that circle. At Delphi, the distance from the centre of the *orchestra* to the front of the first row of seats is 9.95 m and a square drawn within the circle is 14.07 m on each side. Thus the width of the *proskenion* should be 2.92 m: indeed the measurement of the foundation is precisely consistent with that figure. The length of the *skene* is equal to the diameter of the circle. The entire *skene* appears to be displaced by 70 cm to the east vis-à-vis the position of the *theatron*; this anomaly is unexplained.

An idea of the original appearance of the *skene* at Delphi may be gained by comparison with relics in the theatres of Priena and Oropos[9]: in all probability the *proskenion* was 2.70 m in height, 2.92 m wide and 20 m long, with a timber floor at the rear (Fig. 10). The floor at the front rested on a row of Doric columns, while at the rear it was contiguous with the front edge of the *skene*. Actors are believed to have performed on the floor of the *proskenion* (*logeion*), while the musicians and chorus were in the *orchestra* (we should bear in mind that at this time the role of the chorus was much diminished).[10]

In Hellenistic times, the *skene* was a two-storey

[9] Bieber 1961, 108-112; Izenour 1977, 11-13.
[10] Nicoll 1961, 23-30.

building of simple form, with a floor on the level of the *proskenion*. The foundations at Delphi indicate that the stairs from the lower to the upper level were located in the middle of the western end. The upper floor (*episkenion*) had large gaps from floor to ceiling in the side facing the audience. According to sources, at this time painted backdrops were used during performances; these were installed within gaps on the upper floor or between the pillars of the *proskenion*.

The foundations also show that the *skene* comprises three parts. Due to the slope of the territory, it was necessary to construct transverse walls to reinforce the 20-metre-long building. This may also be an indication that a side stage or *paraskenia* of some kind stood on either side of the stage.

All manmade structures are subject to the fundamental requirement of functionality and it is in the nature of a theatre to be a setting for dramatic performance. The view has sometimes been put forward that the setting alone is insignificant; and it is true that if the subject of a play is commonplace, it does not matter where it is staged. The Greek tragedies, however, share the quality of addressing fresh yet classic themes, with supernatural powers always close by in the shape of the gods.

In the summer of 1963, I was fortunate enough to see the Greek actor Aspasia Papathanassiou in the roles of Electra and Medea in the packed theatre at Delphi.[11] Her quietest whisper could be clearly heard throughout the theatre, soft and effortless. And as the play progressed, the theatre itself – the stones, the cliffs, everything – resounded with her despair and unhappiness. In other words, the play confirmed that the acoustics of the Delphi theatre are outstanding – and indeed the ancient Greeks are known to have placed great emphasis on this aspect of architecture. When Papathanassiou played the same two roles again shortly afterwards in The Royal Theatre in Copenhagen, the difference was obvious. In Delphi, the gods moved freely through the drama and the theatre, while in Copenhagen they provided no resonance, leaving the characters of the tragedy forsaken.

In 1975, I was commissioned, along with two colleagues, to design a new City Theatre in Reykjavík. While there is a great difference between a modern theatre in Europe's northernmost capital and the ancient Greek theatre at Delphi, I intend to point out some aspects of the former building which have Greek roots (Fig. 11).

In Icelandic terms, the theatre is large, with two auditoria of different sizes. One seats 150-220, depending on how the seating is arranged, while the other has fixed seating for 520. The larger auditorium is the subject of my remarks. The rows of seats are curved, arranged concentrically around a large revolving stage which is set into the stage floor. The auditorium is far from being as open in form as the traditional Greek *theatron*, but by comparison with many modern theatres, where the auditorium is either rectangular or horseshoe-shaped, the audience seating area is certainly more open. And on closer scrutiny the module is seen to be the same as that used by the Greeks for each sector of the *theatron*, precisely 30°. The auditorium comprises two such modules, totalling 60°. Entrance points are arranged in a similar fashion to those at Delphi: two for the lower section of the auditorium, and two for the upper rows. The entrances for the lower level are via aisles two metres wide (a kind of *parados*), formed by displacing the side walls. As at Delphi, the uppermost rows are truncated at both ends by walls which meet at an angle of 60°, symmetrically with the front part of the auditorium. The upper entrances are placed between these walls and the curved rear wall. The front edge of the stage is curved, with a radius double that of the revolving stage.

Unlike many modern theatres, the auditorium has no dress circle or balcony, but comprises a continuous ranking of rows. There is no *diazoma* or horizontal aisle separating the lower from the upper auditorium: access to all seating is from stairs at the ends of the rows, along the side walls. The seating rows are all equally spaced, 88 cm apart, but the angle of slope increases toward the top of the auditorium. The steeper pitch is achieved in three stages of more-or-less equal width. The rise between each row and the next is a multiple of 15

[11] The productions were given by Piraikon Theatron under the direction of Dimitrios Rondiris.

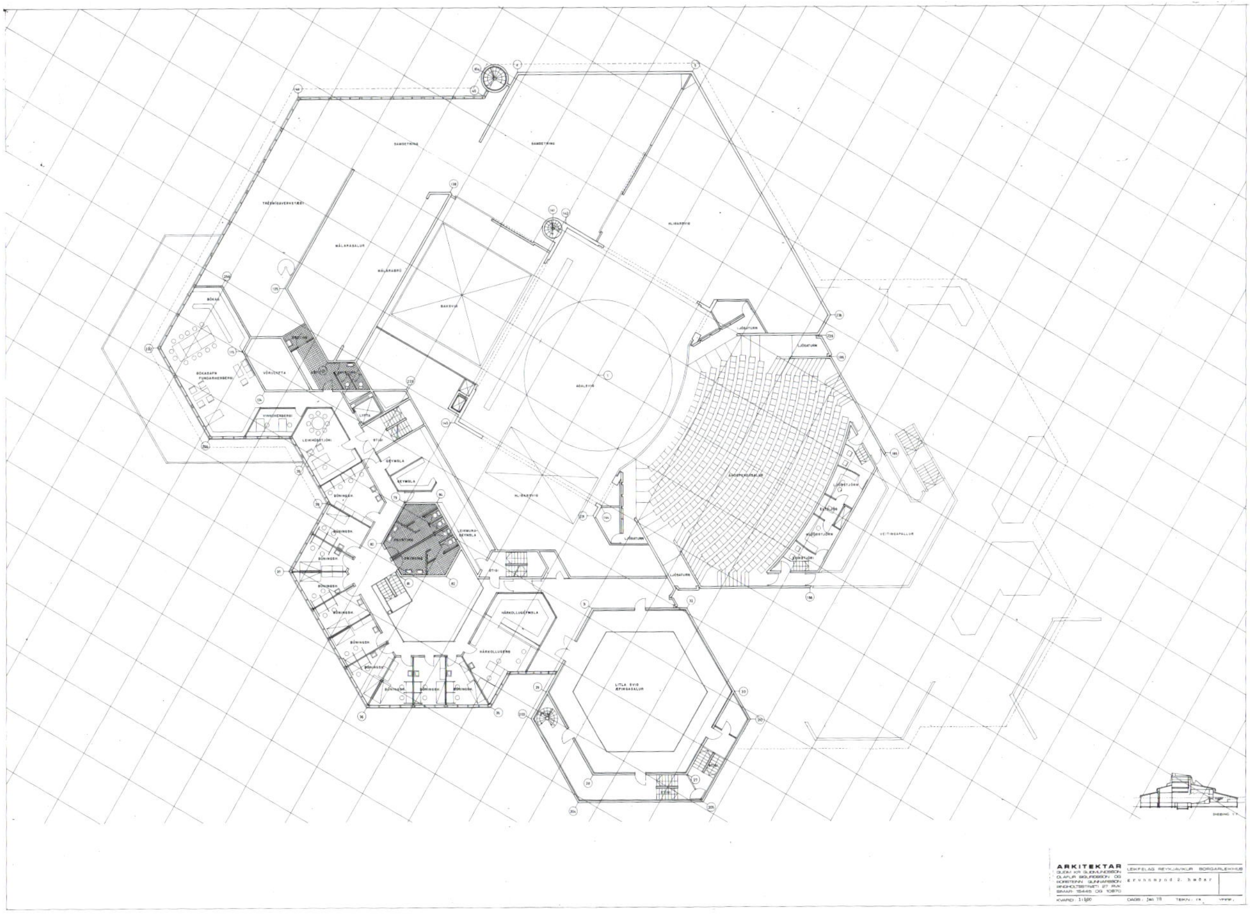

Fig. 11. Plan of Reykjavik City Theatre.

cm. At the lowest level the rise is 15 cm, in the central section 30 cm and in the uppermost part 45 cm, or in terms of degrees the angle of slope is 9.5, 19 and 27. One contrivance remains to be mentioned: the rows of seats are not horizontal, but are designed with a curvature, so they are lowest in the centre and highest at the ends. This enhances the audience's line of sight and their sense of togetherness (Fig. 12).

In Iceland an open-air theatre is not a practical proposition. But the use of dark-blue seating and delicate lighting is intended to create an ambiance of sitting out of doors under a starry sky. After a quarter of a century's use, the Reykjavík City Theatre has won a reputation for being suitable for staging musicals and ballet, as well as classic plays by such playwrights as Shakespeare and Molière, not to mention the three great masters of Greek tragedy.

With a population of 320,000, Iceland is classified as a small nation. And although more than

Fig. 12. Auditorium of Reykjavik City Theatre.

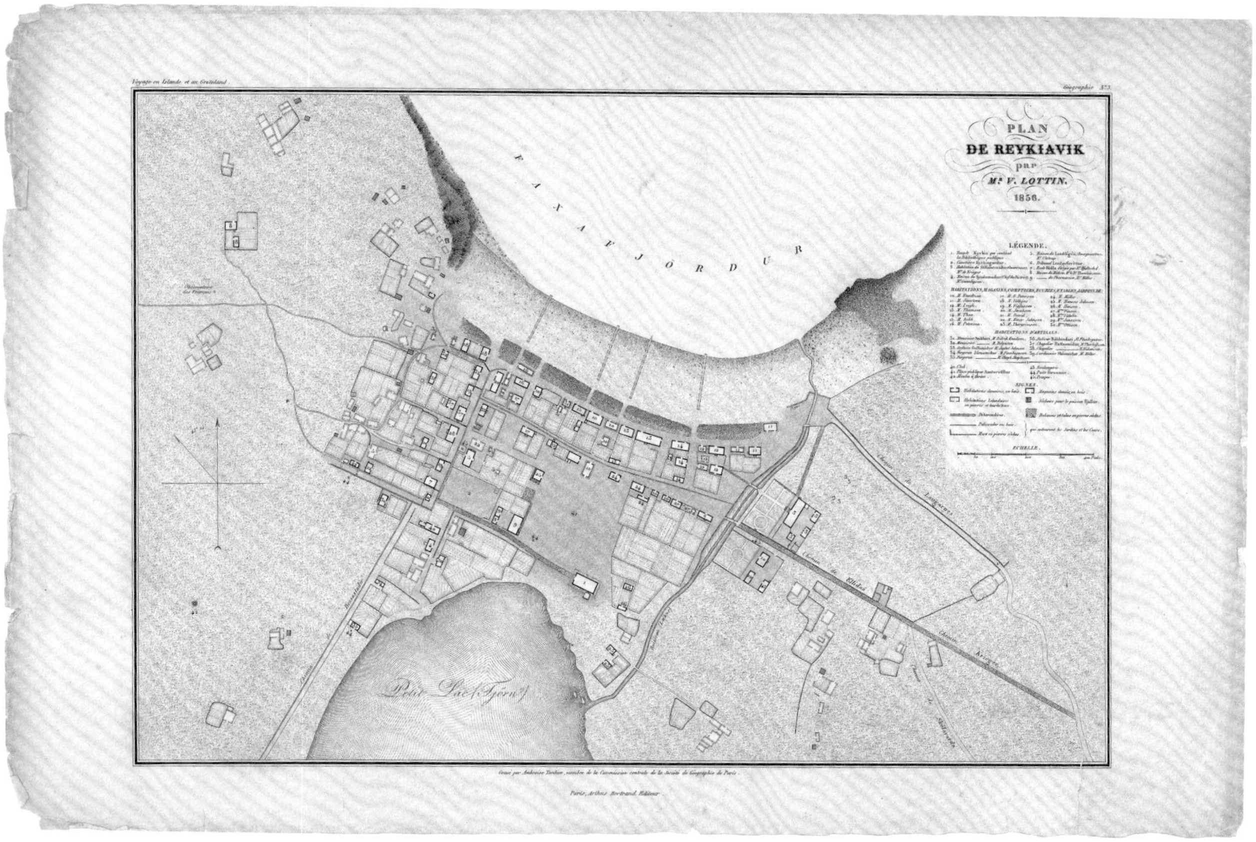

Fig. 13. Map of Reykjavik city 1836. Survey and plans by Victor Lottin.

half the population live in and around the capital, Reykjavík, it is no metropolis. In 1835 and 1836 a group of French scientists visited Iceland on an expedition. At that time Reykjavík consisted of about 50 buildings, of which two were built of stone – the church and the jailhouse – while the rest were wood or turf structures (Fig. 13). With this beautiful map of the town, surveyed and drawn in 1836 by the French naval commander and physicist Victor Lottin, and which is the third-oldest map made of Reykjavík, I would like to express my thanks to the French School at Athens and my former mentor, the architect Erik Hansen, for the opportunity I had to survey and draw plans of the theatre in Delphi, many years ago.

Bibliography

Bieber, M., 1961
The History of the Greek and Roman Theatre, Princeton, NJ.

Dyggve, E., 1949
Funktionalismen i amfiteatret, Copenhagen.

Gunnarsson, Þ., 1991
'Leikhúsið í Delfí', in *Grikkland ár og síð* (1991), S.A. Magnússon, K. Árnason, Þ. Þorsteinsson and G.J. Guðmundsson (eds.), Reykjavik, 219-239.

Hansen, E., G. Algreen-Ussing *et al.*, 1975,
Fouilles de Delphes II, Paris.

Homolle, Th. *et al.*, 1902ff.
Les Fouilles de Delphes, Paris.

Izenour, G.C., 1977
Theater Design, New York.

Kirk, F., 1955
'Studier af teatret i Epidaurus', *Arkitekten* 4-5, 58-63.

Lawrence, A.W., 1962
Greek Architecture, London.

Nicoll, A., 1961
The Development of the Theatre, London.

Robertson. D.S., 1959
A Handbook of Greek and Roman Architecture, Cambridge.

The Danish architects and their contribution to ancient and modern architecture

Martin Schmid

During my career at the French School at Athens, I had the opportunity and the good fortune to come into contact with Danish architects, whether indirectly through their projects or through our collaboration on the architectural studies I made for the French School. These collaborations were made possible thanks to the kindness of the man who animated the presence of Danish architects in Greece during the third period of their activity in the country – that is during all of the last half century – Erik Hansen.

My intention is to talk about this period only and I would like to do so in reference to my own experiences on the archaeological sites of Amathus in Cyprus, Delos and Delphi, and Malia in Crete, and in reference to the deep impact these architects had on my own projects and on other French colleagues; and, generally, on the study not only of ancient monuments, but also on modern architecture (Figs. 1-4).

The "Danish school" had the merit of creating conventional symbol standards for drawing

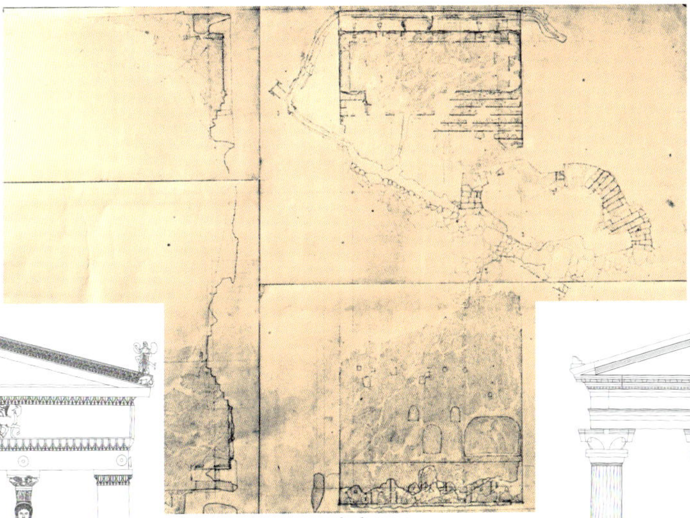

Delphi.
The Fountain of Castalie.
Annelise Bramsnæs.

Delphi.
Treasure of the Siphnians.
Erik Hansen.

Malia. Dighouse.
Søren Harboe.

Amathus. Temple of Aphrodite.
Torben Tyregod Jensen.

Figs. 1-4. Examples of works by Danish architects working for the French School at Athens.

Without hatching

With hatching

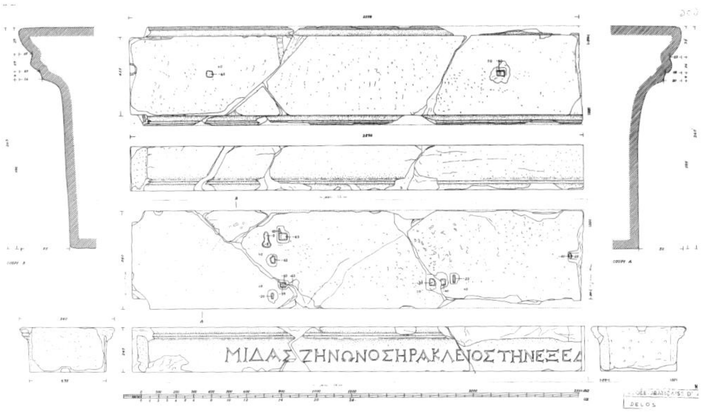

Fig. 5. Delos: Steen Agger 1966.

Fig. 7. Delphi: Karsten Rønnow 1958.

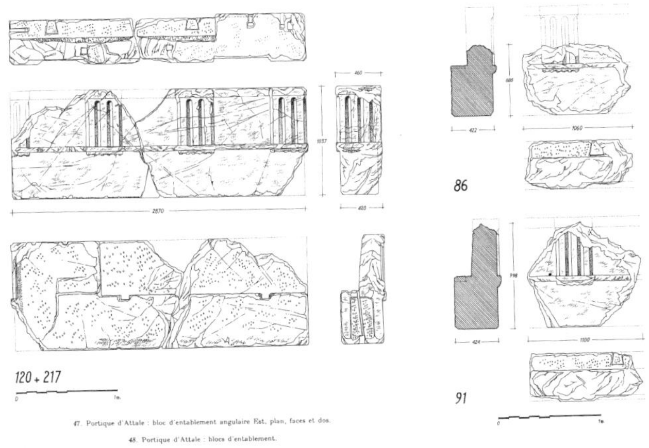

Fig. 6. Delphi: Olivier Callot 1987.

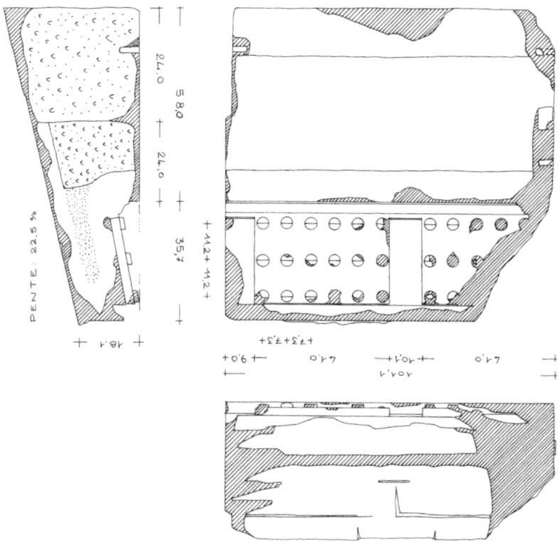

Fig. 8. Delphi: Jean Blécon 1987.

Figs. 5-8. Drawing of two representations of breaks in stones.

ancient monuments and, particularly, symbols for the carving of ancient stones. The drawings and measurements, necessary for study, are made up of a maximum of information represented not only in the most clear, objective, precise and rigorous manner possible, but also in an aesthetic way which it is impossible to remain indifferent to.

The numerous plans, sections, elevations and detail drawings published in some of the remarkable volumes of the *Fouilles de Delphes* such as the treasury of the Siphnians, the Atlas of Delphi or the Palace at Malia, testify to this useful and aesthetic manner of representation.

The fact that, all the same, we find variations in the methods of representation, for example, the use or not of hatching to indicate the broken sections of stones, shows adaptability in respect to the proposed standards. The two methods had their emulators; hatching was used by the French architect Jean Blécon who also adopted the writing of measurements by hand in the publications on the Theban treasury and the Temple of the Marmaria at Delphi, following the manner of Erik Hansen and Karsten Rønnow. I preferred the representation without hatching, so that the broken sections are left white in contrast with the carved parts de-

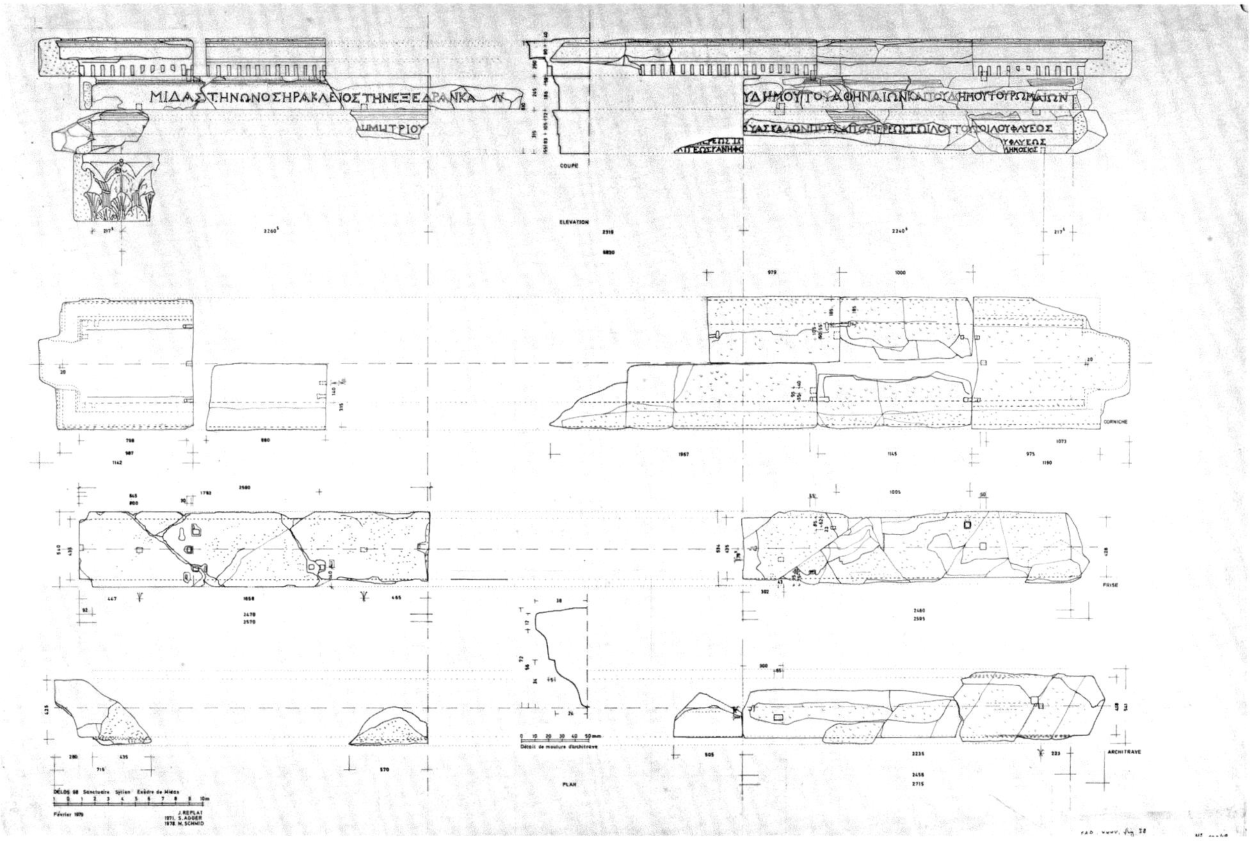

Fig. 9. Delos: sanctuary of the Syrian deity. Graphic reconstruction drawing, Martin Schmid using the drawing of isolated drawings made by Danish architects.

picted by specific symbols, following the example of Steen Agger and others. Another French architect, Olivier Callot used this second method in his drawings at Delphi (Figs. 5-8).

At the very beginning of my work at the French School, I established a design charter based on the Danish model standards, adapting it for different contexts. But as you perhaps know, architects belong to a profession of non-conformists coloured by the well-known "individualism" of the French – and of course I cannot escape this attitude myself. The consequence is that the drawings made and published by different architects are not homogenous; however, we can still recognize the influence of the standard Danish charter.

These standards developed after the first period of the Danish architects' work, that is, from 1908 to 1914, during which the drawings represented the ruins in a realistic manner and a version of which was nevertheless still practised by French architects in the 1980s. Another merit of the "Danish school" is the high level of precision and the quality of the layout drawings. This precision, essential for the study and layout of plans of ancient architecture, is also useful for the graphic reconstruction of the monuments. In this way, the isolated architectural elements drawn by the Danish architects could easily be integrated into the general reconstruction of the monument, as in the sanctuary of the Syrian deity on the island of Delos (Fig. 9).

The site of Malia

The layout of the palace at Malia in Crete by Elga Andersen is so precise that it was easy to set up the foundations of a new shelter over the east magazines as these foundations were placed behind and

Fig. 10. Malia: the roofing of the east magazines of the Palace on the left, the Crypt and Quarter *Mu*. Photo: Christophe Gaston.

Fig.11. Malia, the east magazines of the Palace.

Fig. 12. Malia, the Crypt.

in the axis of the portico pillars. It was not as easy to set up the foundations of another shelter over the crypt, the plan of which was drawn by a French technician. The plan was so inaccurate that I was obliged not only to draw a new plan of the ruins, but also to modify the drawing of the new shelter (Figs. 10-12).

The drawings of the palace by Elga Andersen are so perfect that it was possible to integrate into her plan the remains discovered during further excavations. Each stone of the palace is drawn in its real place and even the flagstones of the great courtyard can be easily recognised. Such an approach testifies to an extraordinary intellectual honesty (Fig. 13).

Confronted with plans made by architects from different nationalities on several archaeological sites, I can assert that the only plans I could trust entirely were these of Danish architects. In saying this I do not mean to give you the impression that we have no good French architects, but I will simply mention that they are not very fond of measurements. You will therefore understand why I called Erik Hansen for assistance in sending me students interested in participating in the study of a Roman Temple – the temple dedicated to the deity Aphrodite situated at the summit of a hill dominating the sea at Amathus in Cyprus.

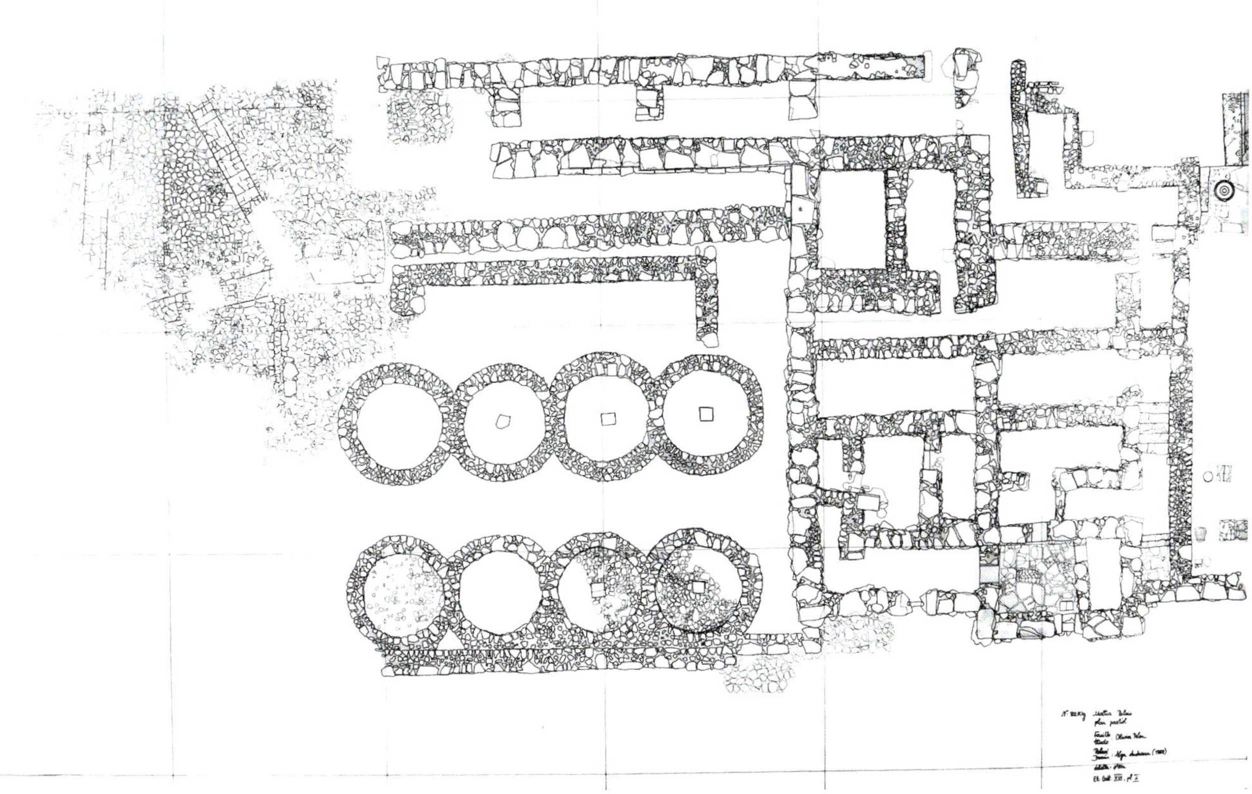

Fig. 13. Malia south west part of the Palace; drawing by Elga Andersen.

The site of Amathus (Fig. 14)

Two students of Erik Hansen succeeded one another, first Lena Skafte-Skov, followed by Torben Thyregod Jensen, who participated first as a student, then as a qualified architect during the years 1995-2005, with an interruption of several years. Torben measured and drew numerous architectural members of the temple (Fig. 15) and then collaborated in the study of the monument. My wish to maintain this collaboration until the end could only partially be realised and not without difficul-

Fig. 14. Amathus: the site.
Photo: Pierre Aupert.

Fig.15 Amathus: the Sanctuary of Aphrodite Photo: Pierre Aupert..

Fig. 16. Torben Thyregod Jensen measuring a column drum.

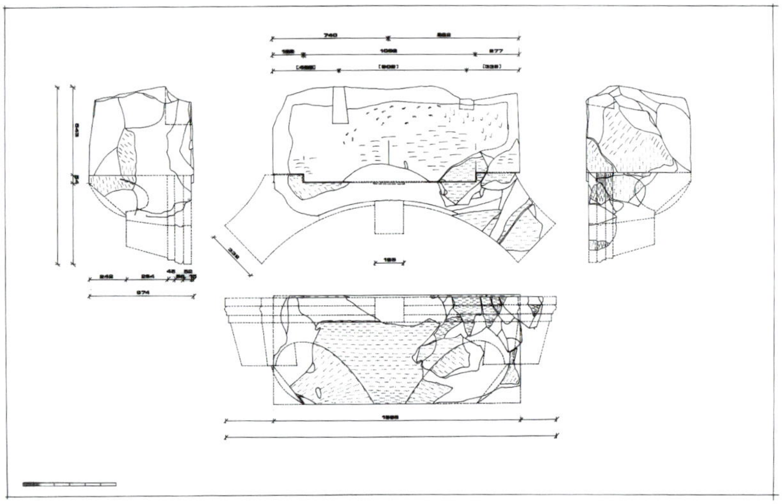

Fig. 17. Drawing of a Nabatean capital by Torben Tyregod Jensen.

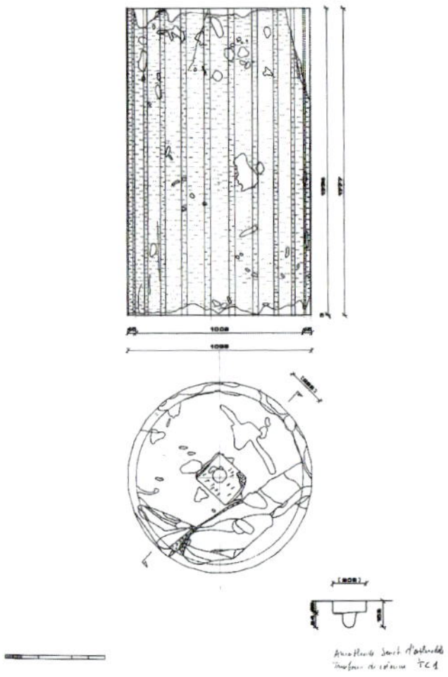

Fig. 18. Drawing of a colume drumm by Torben Tyregod Jensen.

Fig.19. Lene Skafte-Skov is seen to the right. Photo: Antoine Hermary.

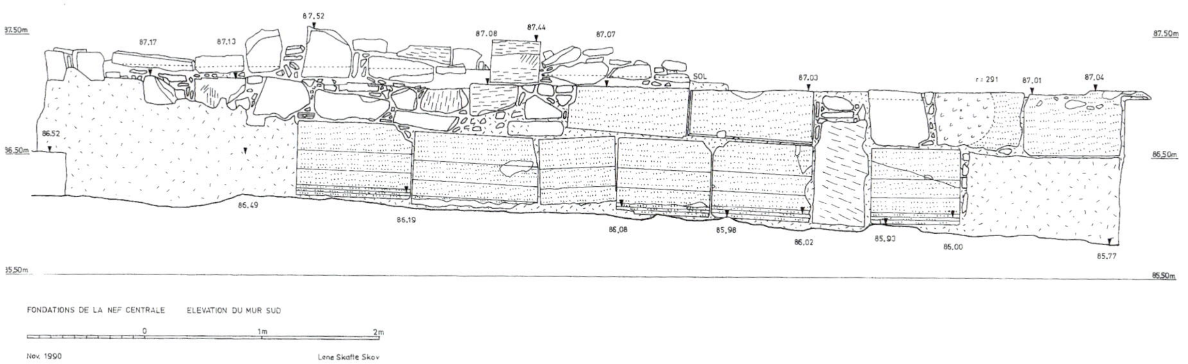

Fig. 20. Drawing of reemployed stones by Lene Skafte-Skov.

ties as the former director was not in agreement. As a consequence, I had to find funds in Cyprus to continue the collaboration for one more year. After that I had to continue alone for some years. I was very disappointed to end the collaboration at the very time when Torben had become fully involved in the restoration project and when his knowledge of the matter had reached the highest degree (Figs. 16-18).

Lene Skafte-Skov (Fig. 19) was the first Danish architecture student to participate in the Amathus excavations. During two campaigns in 1990-91, she measured and drew architectural fragments of monuments from the sanctuary of Aphrodite, such as Doric capitals from a Hellenistic portico and pieces of the temple that had been reused in the foundations of the Christian basilica built its stone. Her drawings were worthy of the reputation for precision and quality achieved by the "Danish school" (Fig. 20).

During the numerous campaigns spent together with Torben in Amathus measuring the stones, we had the opportunity to talk about aspects of life in antiquity and today, including the aesthetic architectural creation of all periods, in a stimulating exchange of thoughts – a positive exchange which brought not only a high level of efficiency to the study, but also resulted in a genuine friendship.

I am therefore very happy to thank the two directors for having invited Torben to this seminar so that he can express his thoughts about the importance of the work done, a work which always begins with tiresome measuring before the interesting part can start, that is, to find the original position of each stone and to restore the monument. His contribution to the study was of great benefit as he checked my proposals and made new proposals for the graphic reconstruction of the east and west facades, and for the theoretical geometric features of the Nabatean capital. It is therefore so very regrettable that this collaboration, this connection between the French school and the Danish academy, did not receive the consideration it deserved from the former director of the EFA.

The site of Delphi

The drawings of the sanctuary of Apollo at Delphi by Gregers Algreen-Ussing and Annelise Bramsnæs are more than a masterpiece – they have been, are,

Fig. 21. The theatre of Delphi.

Fig. 22. View of the temple.

Fig. 23. Reconstruction of monuments in Delphi.

Fig. 24. Reconstruction of monuments in Delphi.

and will continue to be, so useful for the study of the monuments and the site, that they constitute an achievement we can never praise enough. To draw the ruins of the monuments at Delphi situated in this natural and magnificent setting, in a place somehow magical – a place which emanates an impression of divinity – certainly satisfying, but this in no way lessens the tremendous work done by Thorstein Gunnarsson in drawing the irregular tiers of this wonderful theatre (Fig. 21 and this volume p. 69-79, figs. 6-7).

The temple of Apollo (Fig. 22) is another monument represented in the Atlas book of Delphi, the plans of which constitute the basis and reference for all studies and interventions on the site.

As I participated in the study of the monuments situated on the first part of the sacred way (Figs. 23-24), I constantly used the plans and sections of

Fig. 25. Malia: aerial view of the site

Fig. 26. The finished dighouse 1962.

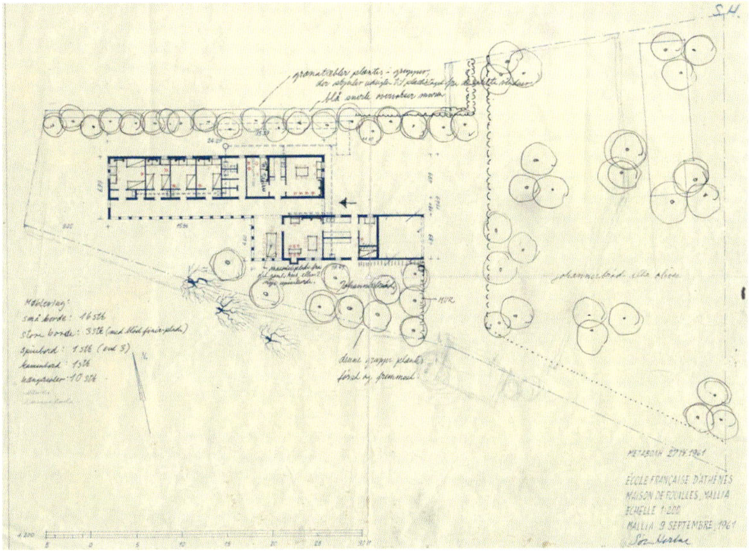

Fig. 27. Plan of the dighouse 1961: architect Søren Harboe.

the Atlas made by a team of Danish architects, for the study and for the restoration and anastylosis of the monuments. The graphic three-dimensional reconstruction drawings made by the French architect J. Laragné rely on the same drawings.

Considering the quantity and the quality of the drawings produced by Danish architects over a period of a century, the small number of publications signed jointly with the archaeologist is regrettable; these publications are mostly from the third period, for in earlier periods the volume with the texts was usually signed by the archaeologists and the volume of drawings by the architects, as for example in the case of Kai Gottlob in the publication of the tholos at Delphi. The drawings were mostly used by the archaeologists, but also by architects as they mainly depicted the actual state of the ruins or isolated pieces of architecture belonging to the monuments. It is perhaps one of the reasons why they are so praised by the archaeologists who still use the plans sometimes in order to illustrate their texts.

Modern architecture

The Danish architects collaborating with the French school were not only responsible for the ancient monuments, but were also creating modern architecture as was the case at the site of Malia (Fig. 25).

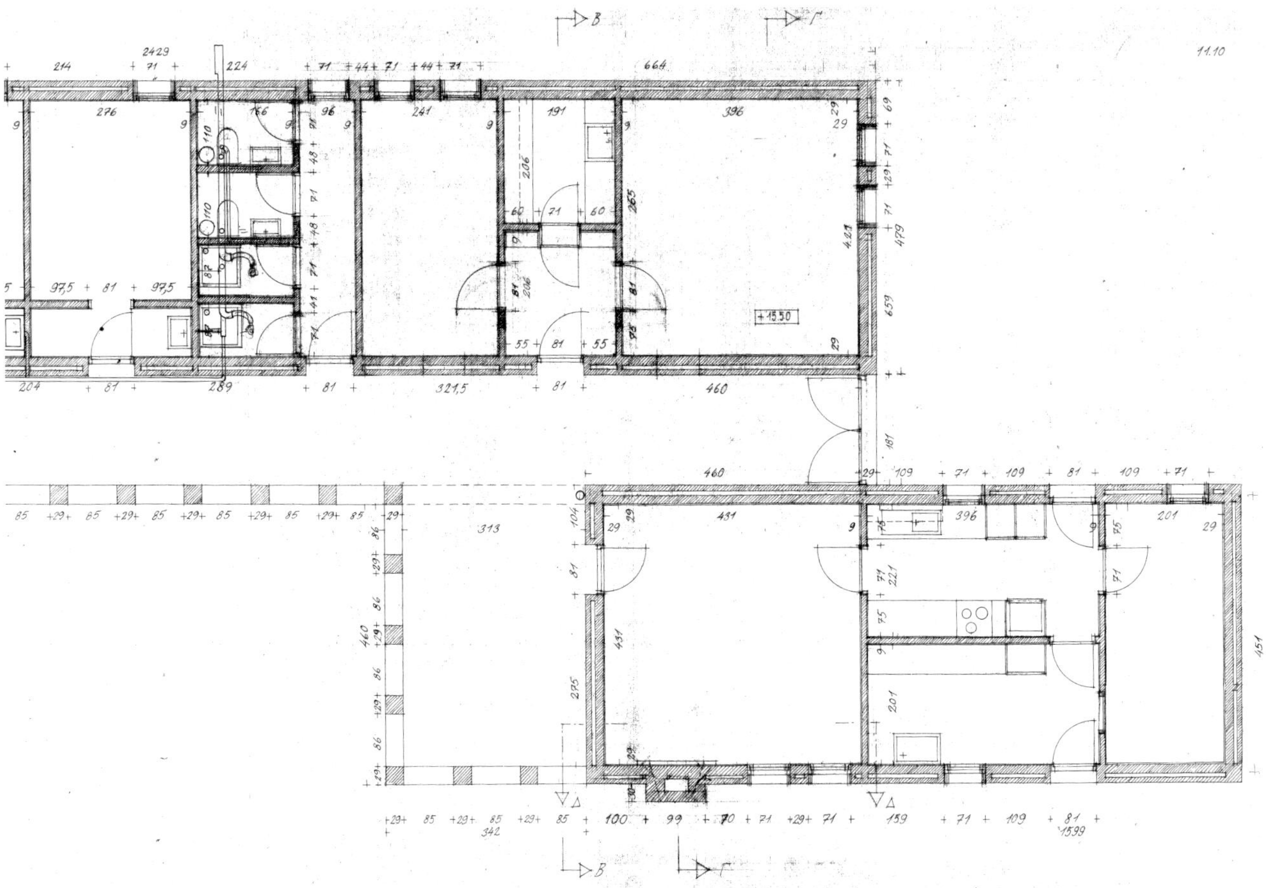

Fig. 28. The dighouse: architect Søren Harboe 1961-62. Partial plan.

Fig. 29. The dighouse: architect Søren Harboe 1961-62. Floor in library.

It was the architect Søren Harboe who in 1961-62 designed and built, in the middle of the archaeological site, the dig house surrounded by a garden (Figs. 26-27), which made the house a pleasant and charming place to live in. The house has two sections connected in the middle by the entrance and the covered veranda which forms an exterior living room for the summer. The rooms oriented northwards open to a portico accessing the bathroom, the drawing office, the photo laboratory transformed into a storage room, and the library, all on one side. The opposite side of the portico accommodates the interior living room with fireplace, the kitchen, the laundry and the service room (Figs. 28-29). The house is built with open brickwork that was just whitewashed without coating, lending the building a special character, and the sloping roof is covered with yellow tiles. A garage that was designed as part of the building could not be constructed, which changed the balance of the two buildings.

The same architect also paid detailed attention to the interior design, such as the flooring – particularly the flooring of the library, which was ex-

Fig. 30. The photo tower: Søren Harboe architect.

ecuted with great care (Fig. 29) – and even designed the furniture, beds and tables. The famous Danish lamps that were used were imported from Denmark.

Søren Harboe also produced the plans of a building for the storage of archaeological material, in 1964-65. The construction was built under the supervision of Knud Larsen, another Danish architect I met once in the 70s, who was also the author of detail drawings for objects such as doors and storage furniture for sherds and vases, made of wooden drawers placed in a metal structure – a very clever and practical system. The original construction of 1964 was slightly modified by Harboe in 1965 by removing the interior pillars, thus providing more space for studying the excavated material on large tables placed along the windows. This pattern of storage works so well that I reproduced it when building a new storage magazine beside the former, in 1992; the only modifications I made were to add a room for restoration and to increase the window size.

Harboe achieved what every architect would like to achieve: a true "tour de force" which completely satisfied the needs of the user on both the functional and aesthetic level. He also designed a touristic pavilion which, however, was not built. We also owe to him the tripod photo tower placed here near Quartier Mu (Fig. 30), an exceptionally well preserved monument discovered in 1966, the drawings of which were done at the very beginning by the Danish architects, Ole Jappe, Sten Holbæk and Jacob Erlangsen.

Future collaboration

Today we are no longer in the same position as in the 19th century, when architects studied ancient monuments in order to use the models for planning modern buildings, however, the study of their proportions, the movement of the light and shadow on their facades, their colours, their material, is not without interest for the planners of today.

Is this enough to motivate young students of architecture to come to Greece to work on programs of the French school for a short period, without the assurance of being involved in the study until the end?

Certainly topographical instruments have evolved a great deal since the Atlas was made – instruments such as total stations, GPS, photogrammetry, orthophotography and laser planning, providing great assistance in measuring the ruins. In this respect, the collaboration of topographers is necessary, permitting the architects more time to concentrate on architectural issues. Of course, candidate architect students need to be trained in the relevant computer applications.

The French School would greatly benefit its study of ancient monuments by creating new appointments for one or more architects, as members of the school on the same level as the member archaeologists, historians, epigraphers and modern historians. It would thus be possible to create an appointment for a French member and another for a Danish member, as was once the practice, continuing to invite trainee students to be supervised by these members, whether French, within the existing convention with the architectural school of Strasbourg, or Danish, within a convention to be created with the Royal Academy of Fine Arts in Copenhagen.

This seminar, which follows the exhibition organized by the Danish Institute and the French School of Athens, gives us the opportunity to consider the different aspects of a future collabo-

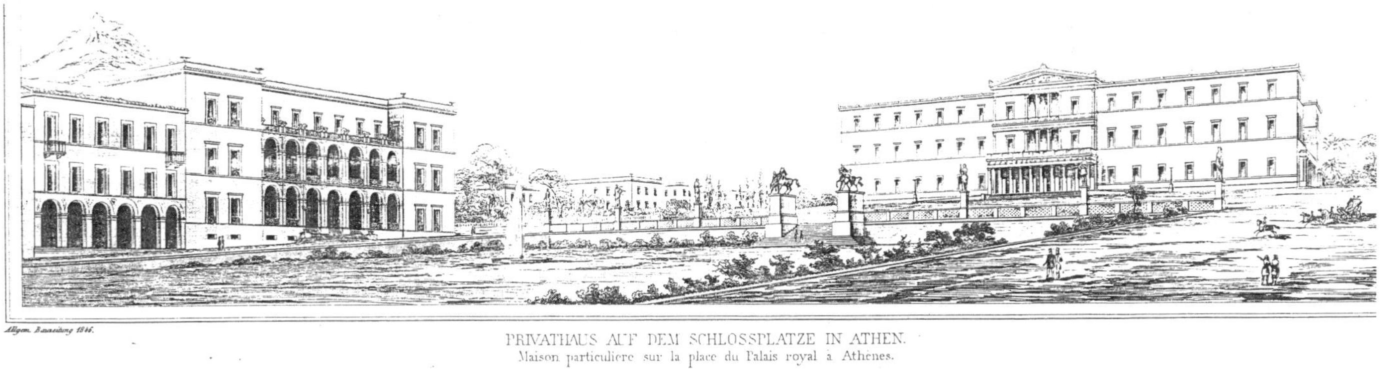

Fig. 31. "le palais majestueux" housing the French school of Athens from 1856 to 1873: architect Theophile Hansen 1842.

ration of Danish architects and students with the French School. It is also, and mainly, the opportunity – and I thank Erik Hallager for his initiative – to pay homage to the Danish architects who taught me so much, to express my gratitude to those I did not know but whose perfect drawings made my work easier – Steen Agger, Ole Jappe, Sten Holbæk, Niels Christofersen, to those who collaborated in my studies – Torben Thyregod Jensen and Lene Skafte-Skov – and, last but not least, to Erik Hansen who sent me his best students.

What an auspicious omen it was for the presence of the Danish architects at the French School that from 1856 to 1873, that institution was located on the main square of Athens (Figs. 31-32) – Constitution (Syntagma) Square – in the majestic palace that was built in fact by a Danish architect, the very famous Theophil Hansen, creator of the National Library and the Academy of Athens.

Fig. 32. The main facade of the building: architect Theophile Hansen 1842.

Conclusion

Beyond the fruitful collaboration of Danish architects in the studies and work of the French School that spanned a whole century, what can we expect for the future?

We can wish that there is still goodwill from both directors, that is, of the Royal Academy of Fine Arts in Copenhagen and the French School of Athens, to sign an agreement for the future, to the benefit of both institutions, assuring that the architects will regain the role and the status that are rightfully theirs.

Conversations with a French architect – present meets past, creating future*

Experience and thoughts – free after open lectures in Athens and Copenhagen autumn/winter 2008

Torben Thyregod Jensen

This is not just about archaeology and architecture.

This is a personal reflection upon how important co-creation is and always will be, if we want significant cultural improvements in life.

Background

Copenhagen

In 1994, at the Royal Academy of Fine Art, School of Architecture, I had the good fortune to have Erik Hansen as a teacher. It was at the end of my studies and I decided to enrol at the Institute 1, specialising in the restoration of our built heritage, a vital but neglected part of architectural education. The department was directed by Professor Hans Munk Hansen, which had a unique group of teachers attached and was, therefore, a dream scenario from a student's perspective. The unique capacity and the level of Erik Hansen's work was unknown to me, to most students, as well as to a broader audience and, unfortunately, still is. The classical measuring of historical architecture is the basis for all understanding and later studies and a discipline that has been practised and sophisticated by Erik Hansen to the highest level.

After a semester on the skills of measuring, I was invited to contact architect Martin Schmid from l´École française d´Athènes regarding the possibility of supporting the French campaign at Amathus in the southern part of Cyprus.

Amathus

In April 1995 I arrived in Cyprus for the first time. It was unseasonably cold, but green and colourful due to spring. The house of excavation was situated on a hillside in the village of Ayius Thyconas, near the actual site at Amathus. The house was beautifully shaped like a shell around an inner garden and would be my home for the coming month – and many more to come.

The site of Amathus, an ancient kingdom naturally placed on the top of a small mountain, is protected towards north, east and west by steep cliffs and towards south by the sea. The Kingdom has hosted and attracted people throughout time. Evidence can be seen from the very early Archaic period to the much later Byzantine period with more or less significant remains.

The overall excavation has been on going since the 1970´s and each year teams apply and compete for budgets to make campaigns, excavating a certain historical period. The improvement of each excavation, therefore, depends on the year's budget and a steady progressive flow is obviously difficult.

The campaign I enrolled in was the excavation of The Temple of Aphrodite, one of the most spectacular Roman temples on the island of Cyprus. Professor Antoine Hermary conducted the Roman excavation and Martin Schmid was responsible

* Acknowledgement: To my beloved family for their support and patience and to my dear niece Helena Newbold and colleague Lena Chawes for proof reading. All images are by the author.

Fig. 1. Cornice stones belonging to the north-west entablature – the best preserved part of the temple.

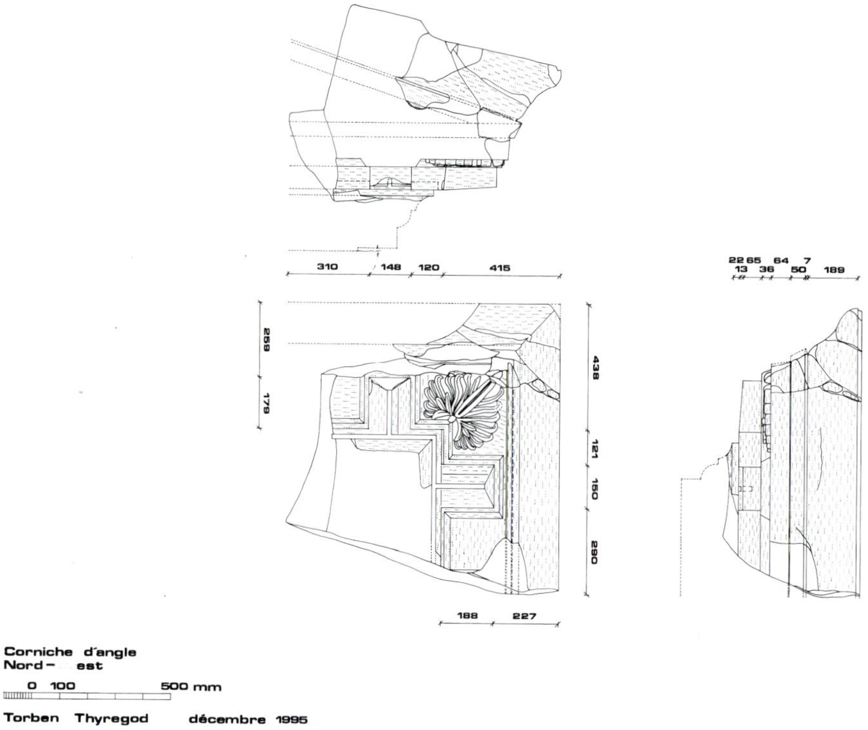

Fig. 2. Angle cornice stone belonging to the north-west entablature (ink on foil).

"In classical time, a temple was the ultimate symbol of humility and respect for something bigger than us, something that per definition cannot be reached by man. To praise Aphrodite seems logical – as small as we are, we can just assign ourselves to the most powerful in life – Love and beauty".

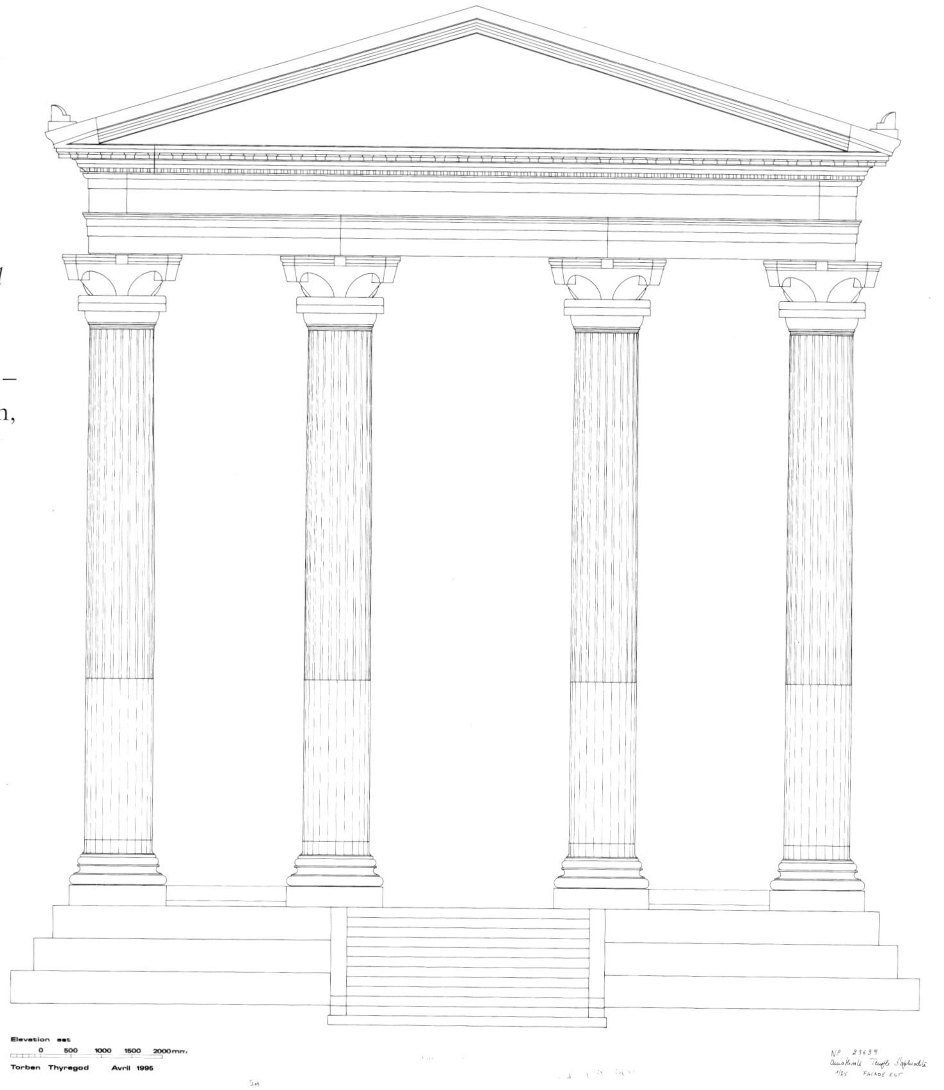

Fig. 3. Temple of Aphrodite – Front elevation. (Early sketch, pencil on foil).

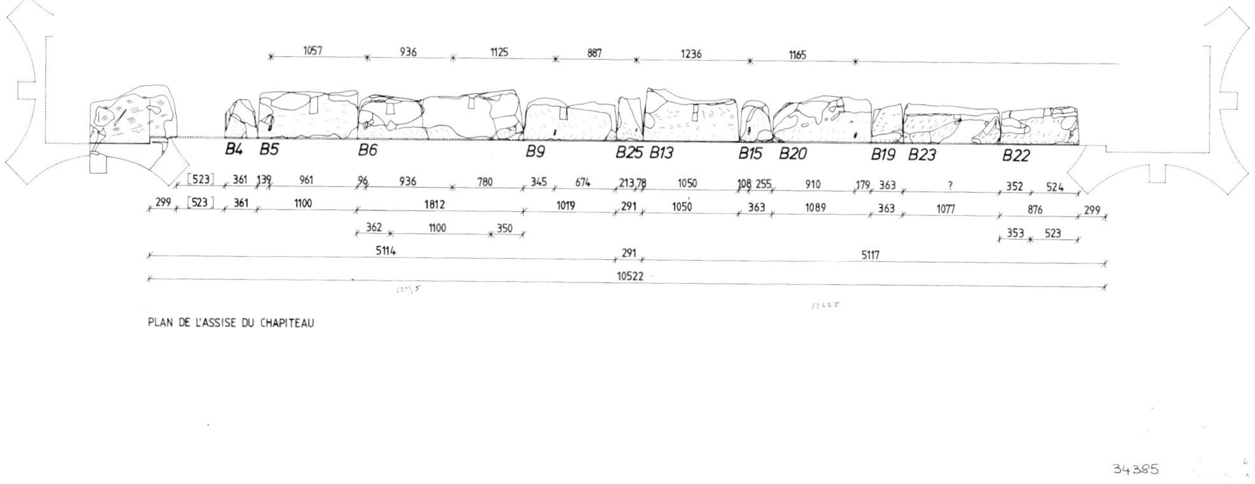

Fig. 4. Plan drawing, capital layer. North-west gable (ink on foil).

"Stones link time and culture"

Fig. 5. Very clearly evidence of cramp holes. Cramps that tightens two architrave stones together. North-west entablature.

"Breakfast"

Fig. 6. Martin Schmid in the drawing room, house of excavation.

for the architectural studies, including complete measuring of the site as well as all of the stones. My job was to assist Martin Schmid in the measuring as well as in the general study of the temple, aimed at an overall publication and maybe also a potential reconstruction. Historical evidence means a great deal to the local self-image and in the village of Agios Tychonas, the owner of the land where the temple is situated, was certainly interested in a potential reconstruction.

My Danish predecessor in this exciting job, Lene Skafte Skov, had made important measurements and drawings, but a lot was still to be done. For that reason, the first months were one big "tour de force" of measuring stones to get the right basic material and knowledge for continuous studies. (Figs. 1-5)

During many hours, working with specific stones on site, as well as at the house of excavation, one begins to reflect. Parallel with the overall task, deeper thoughts begin to occur.

For what purpose are we unearthing history?
Do we really want to understand the past with the capacity to improve the future?

Can I make a difference?

"Before departure for a conference in Nicosia"

Fig. 7. Very good colleagues and friends in the drawing room of the house of excavation, Agios Tychonas, Cyprus. From left Professor Thierry Petit, Professor Antoine Hermary and my genuine friend and mentor, architect Martin Schmid.

Conversations with a French architect

Meeting another person can change one's life!

Very seldom in life does one find a person to reflect upon. Often conversations are superficial, without any deeper meaning, or only represent a certain aspect of a larger potential. Life often passes by without using one's true capacity to think and communicate thoughts. It is in fruitful conversation magic occurs. Martin Schmid is indeed a reflective person. (Figs. 6 and 7).

During many campaigns and, therefore, many months on site at Amathus or in the house of excavation, Martin Schmid and I developed a kind of mutual understanding. Hours and hours of study and conversation concerning architecture and ancient life lead to more general and philosophical conversations.

Conversations were about people, about culture and about our relationship with nature – conversations were about CONTEXT.

Knowledge and skill are obviously the basis for all archaeological excavations, but seem to become inadequate if not used with an onwards progressive perspective. If we were able to communicate our findings in both present and future contexts, balancing as a whole between nature and culture, there may be a more harmonious future. (Fig. 8)

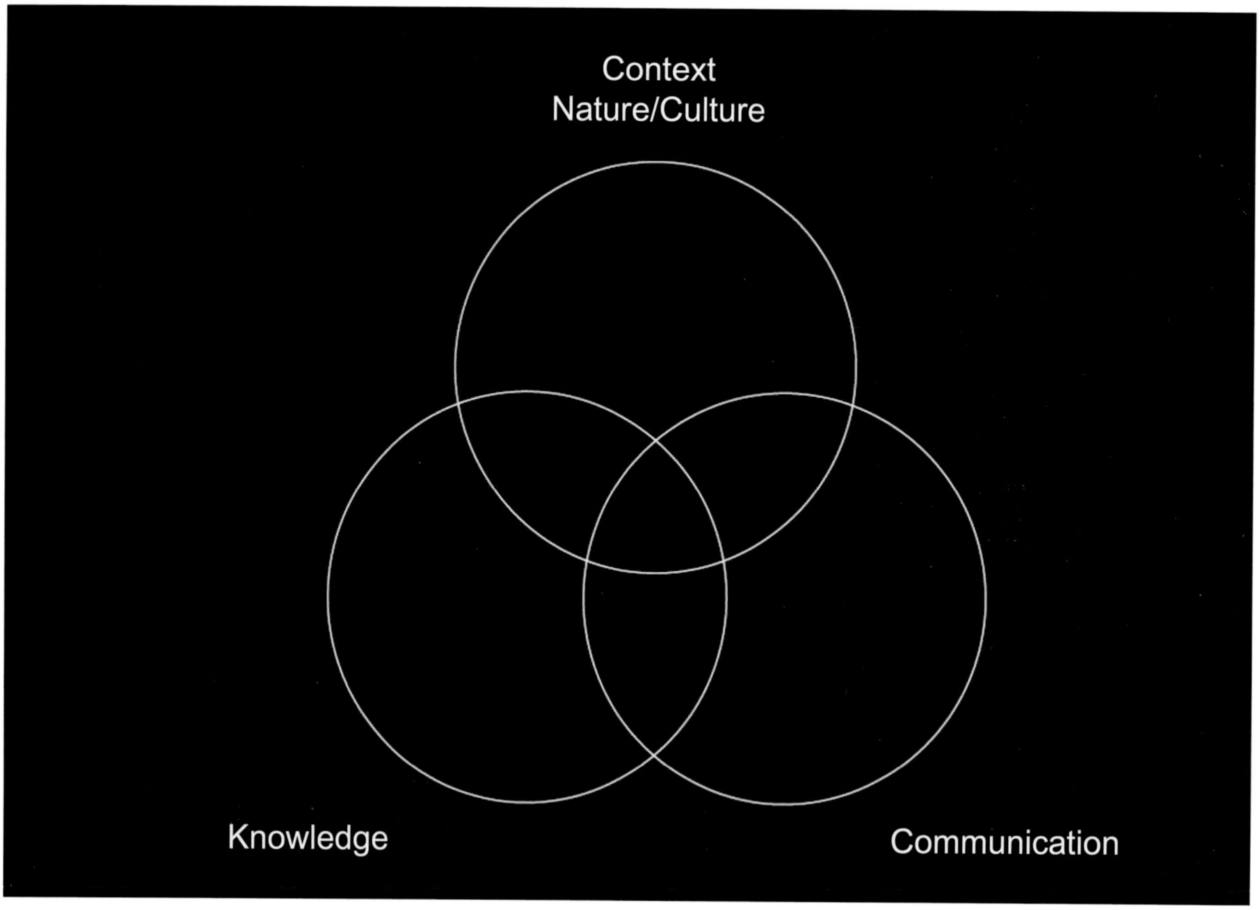

"A simple generic model".

Fig. 8. A similar model was the reason for a conference held in Bucharest; the theme was "Architecture as awareness in time".

Basically, it seems like people are striving for answers rather than questions. Answers, regardless of quality, often seem better than any question. Answers give a certain satisfaction, a kind of fullness, the end of something. However, these answers are often given out of context, without any significant improving effect, sometimes even detaching.

Perhaps we could think and work differently? Perhaps we could start to learn from past experiences, simply by having another focus or even no "focus" at all, but a holistic perspective?

The past may provide some answers. Why did some cultures prosper and others not?

"An exercise" – One could ask oneself why.

Every morning we could perform a small exercise by asking ourselves why.

Why am I here on this wonderful planet?

A simple exercise could then be performed in addition to other doings – a personal daily "*litmus test*". Not only a test for our professional life, but also for our life in general. The outcome might be more than just "the common and so expected talk about producing". Instead we could achieve a kind of "honest producing" according to human needs and time.

"Transparency"

Fig. 9. Stream near Caledonia Falls, Cyprus.

This daily exercise could then be performed in three steps. Each step would be a stepping stone to the next, and an ideal situation would be if the outcome of all three questions had the highest relevance and validity.

Why? – Beauty and Love

If everything we did was based on love of our surroundings and focused on creating more love through beauty, in all its aspects.

This is in no way new. Most past cultures understood the necessity of love and beauty and actually praised these aspects that are so vital to life. All people, without any exception, have beauty and love as their primary marker in life, sometimes neglected or hidden, but impossible to kill. Today, beauty and love have very little impact on our physical surroundings as well as our mental life (Fig. 9).

The Temple of Aphrodite, for instance is dedicated to the goddess of beauty and love.

"All people in past, present and future strive and will strive for love and beauty. It is the one and only real common "language" that separates humans from animals. One could then wonder why we are not doing our utmost to strive for it."

Fig. 10. Petra Tou Rumiou, southern part of Cyprus.

According to legends she was born "in the womb" of the breaking waves at Petra Tou Rumiou, one of the most beautiful places in Cyprus (Fig. 10).

Why? – Human obligation

If everything we did was based on adding value to an overall objective and thinking in "WE" culture,

"We are standing in front of a crossroad that is bigger than usual. There have been crossroads since the dawn of time, but this time our own impact on our planet seems greater than before, almost out of our hands. We treat our planet badly – polluting the water, air and soil, but also changing our own behaviour at a speed never seen before. Consequences could be catastrophic. On the other hand, man has always had a unique capacity to survive and the beginning of a worldwide understanding seems underway in the wake of COP15 in Copenhagen, despite the overall failure".

Fig. 11. Printed statement on a T-shirt, beach on the northern part of Cyprus.

rather than just in a "ME" culture, we could reach and solve larger challenges.

Soon mankind needs to cooperate on a level never seen before. Our very pressing global predicament in connection with e.g. pollution (CO_2, pesticides, plastic, Nano particles etc.) or our energy supply (fossil fuels versus renewable energy) demands completely new ways of thinking (Fig. 11).

"A staircase is difficult to construct, therefore it is the perfect way to test an apprentice. A beautiful staircase with excellent proportions that is a delight to ascend demands highly educated skills. Sometimes staircases are masterpieces and knowledge as well as tools are often inherited"

Fig. 12. Staircase as seen from below, Budapest, Hungary.

COP15 in Copenhagen was an indication of the new coming.

Why? – Professional obligation

If "everything" we did was based on building upon experienced knowledge, adding new qualified knowledge e.g. "*from father to son*", less disastrous mistakes would be made. Often "modern societies" forget, or even neglect, valuable accumulated knowledge. Sometimes it seems like we are starting from scratch every time and actually giving rewards for not "being qualified".

In traditional Japanese craftsmanship for instance, one can find skill honed over generations to the highest possible level, respecting everything involved in the process. These improvements over time must be common sense to most people, but unfortunately it is not that obvious anymore (Fig. 12).

"Everything is mirrored in water as in history – Everything will return! It is up to man himself, to realize the absence of beauty and love. If we choose ugliness and stupidity, we will get it back, even tenfold"

Fig. 13. River Medway by Aylesford, Kent, England.

Present meets past and creates future

Does past have a future?

Imagine a worldwide vision. Imagine a big funnel. Will it be possible in the near future to systematically funnel everything? Including findings from past cultures? Will it really be possible to learn from carefully selected material and create a more holistic and, therefore, a more harmonious world?

Can history be decisive in this vision? (Figs. 13 and 14).

"Nothing will last for ever. Our past will disappear sooner or later, but as long as we are learning, nothing will be forgotten just improved. The only thing in life that will last for ever is the coming day – what a beautiful day."

Fig. 14. Sunset – view from Amathus towards Limassol, Cyprus.

100 years of cooperation between l´École française d´Athènes and The Royal Academy of Fine Arts, School of Architecture in Copenhagen, is a reality. It could easily be the end of an era, but it could also lead to a new, much stronger and broader cooperation. Besides celebrating, why not use this anniversary to revitalise our cooperation? Why not gather with other equals upon a shared vision?

Present meets past and creates future.

Sites where the Danish architects and students of architecture have worked for the French School at Athens.